The American Judicial System: A Very Short Introduction

T0016599

VERY SHORT INTRODUCTIONS are for anyone wanting a stimulating and accessible way into a new subject. They are written by experts, and have been translated into more than 45 different languages.

The series began in 1995, and now covers a wide variety of topics in every discipline. The VSI library currently contains over 700 volumes—a Very Short Introduction to everything from Psychology and Philosophy of Science to American History and Relativity—and continues to grow in every subject area.

Very Short Introductions available now:

ABOLITIONISM Richard S. Newman
THE ABRAHAMIC RELIGIONS
    Charles L. Cohen
ACCOUNTING Christopher Nobes
ADOLESCENCE Peter K. Smith
THEODOR W. ADORNO
    Andrew Bowie
ADVERTISING Winston Fletcher
AERIAL WARFARE Frank Ledwidge
AESTHETICS Bence Nanay
AFRICAN AMERICAN RELIGION
    Eddie S. Glaude Jr
AFRICAN HISTORY
    John Parker and Richard Rathbone
AFRICAN POLITICS Ian Taylor
AFRICAN RELIGIONS Jacob K. Olupona
AGEING Nancy A. Pachana
AGNOSTICISM Robin Le Poidevin
AGRICULTURE Paul Brassley and
    Richard Soffe
ALEXANDER THE GREAT
    Hugh Bowden
ALGEBRA Peter M. Higgins
AMERICAN BUSINESS HISTORY
    Walter A. Friedman
AMERICAN CULTURAL HISTORY
    Eric Avila
AMERICAN FOREIGN RELATIONS
    Andrew Preston
AMERICAN HISTORY Paul S. Boyer
AMERICAN IMMIGRATION
    David A. Gerber
AMERICAN INTELLECTUAL
    HISTORY
    Jennifer Ratner-Rosenhagen

THE AMERICAN JUDICIAL SYSTEM
    Charles L. Zelden
AMERICAN LEGAL HISTORY
    G. Edward White
AMERICAN MILITARY HISTORY
    Joseph T. Glatthaar
AMERICAN NAVAL HISTORY
    Craig L. Symonds
AMERICAN POETRY David Caplan
AMERICAN POLITICAL HISTORY
    Donald Critchlow
AMERICAN POLITICAL PARTIES
    AND ELECTIONS L. Sandy Maisel
AMERICAN POLITICS
    Richard M. Valelly
THE AMERICAN PRESIDENCY
    Charles O. Jones
THE AMERICAN
    REVOLUTION Robert J. Allison
AMERICAN SLAVERY
    Heather Andrea Williams
THE AMERICAN SOUTH
    Charles Reagan Wilson
THE AMERICAN WEST Stephen Aron
AMERICAN WOMEN'S HISTORY
    Susan Ware
AMPHIBIANS T. S. Kemp
ANAESTHESIA Aidan O'Donnell
ANALYTIC PHILOSOPHY
    Michael Beaney
ANARCHISM Colin Ward
ANCIENT ASSYRIA Karen Radner
ANCIENT EGYPT Ian Shaw
ANCIENT EGYPTIAN ART AND
    ARCHITECTURE Christina Riggs

ANCIENT GREECE Paul Cartledge
THE ANCIENT NEAR EAST
    Amanda H. Podany
ANCIENT PHILOSOPHY Julia Annas
ANCIENT WARFARE
    Harry Sidebottom
ANGELS David Albert Jones
ANGLICANISM Mark Chapman
THE ANGLO-SAXON AGE John Blair
ANIMAL BEHAVIOUR
    Tristram D. Wyatt
THE ANIMAL KINGDOM
    Peter Holland
ANIMAL RIGHTS David DeGrazia
THE ANTARCTIC Klaus Dodds
ANTHROPOCENE Erle C. Ellis
ANTISEMITISM Steven Beller
ANXIETY Daniel Freeman and
    Jason Freeman
THE APOCRYPHAL GOSPELS
    Paul Foster
APPLIED MATHEMATICS
    Alain Goriely
THOMAS AQUINAS Fergus Kerr
ARBITRATION Thomas Schultz and
    Thomas Grant
ARCHAEOLOGY Paul Bahn
ARCHITECTURE Andrew Ballantyne
THE ARCTIC Klaus Dodds and
    Jamie Woodward
ARISTOCRACY William Doyle
ARISTOTLE Jonathan Barnes
ART HISTORY Dana Arnold
ART THEORY Cynthia Freeland
ARTIFICIAL INTELLIGENCE
    Margaret A. Boden
ASIAN AMERICAN HISTORY
    Madeline Y. Hsu
ASTROBIOLOGY David C. Catling
ASTROPHYSICS James Binney
ATHEISM Julian Baggini
THE ATMOSPHERE Paul I. Palmer
AUGUSTINE Henry Chadwick
JANE AUSTEN Tom Keymer
AUSTRALIA Kenneth Morgan
AUTISM Uta Frith
AUTOBIOGRAPHY Laura Marcus
THE AVANT GARDE David Cottington
THE AZTECS David Carrasco
BABYLONIA Trevor Bryce
BACTERIA Sebastian G. B. Amyes

BANKING John Goddard and
    John O. S. Wilson
BARTHES Jonathan Culler
THE BEATS David Sterritt
BEAUTY Roger Scruton
LUDWIG VAN BEETHOVEN
    Mark Evan Bonds
BEHAVIOURAL ECONOMICS
    Michelle Baddeley
BESTSELLERS John Sutherland
THE BIBLE John Riches
BIBLICAL ARCHAEOLOGY
    Eric H. Cline
BIG DATA Dawn E. Holmes
BIOCHEMISTRY Mark Lorch
BIOGEOGRAPHY Mark V. Lomolino
BIOGRAPHY Hermione Lee
BIOMETRICS Michael Fairhurst
ELIZABETH BISHOP
    Jonathan F. S. Post
BLACK HOLES Katherine Blundell
BLASPHEMY Yvonne Sherwood
BLOOD Chris Cooper
THE BLUES Elijah Wald
THE BODY Chris Shilling
NIELS BOHR J. L. Heilbron
THE BOOK OF COMMON PRAYER
    Brian Cummings
THE BOOK OF MORMON
    Terryl Givens
BORDERS Alexander C. Diener and
    Joshua Hagen
THE BRAIN Michael O'Shea
BRANDING Robert Jones
THE BRICS Andrew F. Cooper
THE BRITISH CONSTITUTION
    Martin Loughlin
THE BRITISH EMPIRE Ashley Jackson
BRITISH POLITICS Tony Wright
BUDDHA Michael Carrithers
BUDDHISM Damien Keown
BUDDHIST ETHICS Damien Keown
BYZANTIUM Peter Sarris
CALVINISM Jon Balserak
ALBERT CAMUS Oliver Gloag
CANADA Donald Wright
CANCER Nicholas James
CAPITALISM James Fulcher
CATHOLICISM Gerald O'Collins
CAUSATION Stephen Mumford and
    Rani Lill Anjum

THE CELL Terence Allen and
    Graham Cowling
THE CELTS Barry Cunliffe
CHAOS Leonard Smith
GEOFFREY CHAUCER David Wallace
CHEMISTRY Peter Atkins
CHILD PSYCHOLOGY Usha Goswami
CHILDREN'S LITERATURE
    Kimberley Reynolds
CHINESE LITERATURE Sabina Knight
CHOICE THEORY Michael Allingham
CHRISTIAN ART Beth Williamson
CHRISTIAN ETHICS D. Stephen Long
CHRISTIANITY Linda Woodhead
CIRCADIAN RHYTHMS
    Russell Foster and Leon Kreitzman
CITIZENSHIP Richard Bellamy
CITY PLANNING Carl Abbott
CIVIL ENGINEERING David Muir Wood
CLASSICAL LITERATURE William Allan
CLASSICAL MYTHOLOGY
    Helen Morales
CLASSICS Mary Beard and John Henderson
CLAUSEWITZ Michael Howard
CLIMATE Mark Maslin
CLIMATE CHANGE Mark Maslin
CLINICAL PSYCHOLOGY Susan
    Llewelyn and Katie Aafjes-van Doorn
COGNITIVE BEHAVIOURAL
    THERAPY Freda McManus
COGNITIVE NEUROSCIENCE
    Richard Passingham
THE COLD WAR Robert J. McMahon
COLONIAL AMERICA Alan Taylor
COLONIAL LATIN AMERICAN
    LITERATURE Rolena Adorno
COMBINATORICS Robin Wilson
COMEDY Matthew Bevis
COMMUNISM Leslie Holmes
COMPARATIVE LITERATURE
    Ben Hutchinson
COMPETITION AND ANTITRUST
    LAW Ariel Ezrachi
COMPLEXITY John H. Holland
THE COMPUTER Darrel Ince
COMPUTER SCIENCE Subrata Dasgupta
CONCENTRATION CAMPS Dan Stone
CONFUCIANISM Daniel K. Gardner
THE CONQUISTADORS
    Matthew Restall and
    Felipe Fernández-Armesto

CONSCIENCE Paul Strohm
CONSCIOUSNESS Susan Blackmore
CONTEMPORARY ART
    Julian Stallabrass
CONTEMPORARY FICTION
    Robert Eaglestone
CONTINENTAL PHILOSOPHY
    Simon Critchley
COPERNICUS Owen Gingerich
CORAL REEFS Charles Sheppard
CORPORATE SOCIAL RESPONSIBILITY
    Jeremy Moon
CORRUPTION Leslie Holmes
COSMOLOGY Peter Coles
COUNTRY MUSIC Richard Carlin
CREATIVITY Vlad Glăveanu
CRIME FICTION Richard Bradford
CRIMINAL JUSTICE Julian V. Roberts
CRIMINOLOGY Tim Newburn
CRITICAL THEORY
    Stephen Eric Bronner
THE CRUSADES Christopher Tyerman
CRYPTOGRAPHY Fred Piper and
    Sean Murphy
CRYSTALLOGRAPHY A. M. Glazer
THE CULTURAL REVOLUTION
    Richard Curt Kraus
DADA AND SURREALISM
    David Hopkins
DANTE Peter Hainsworth and
    David Robey
DARWIN Jonathan Howard
THE DEAD SEA SCROLLS
    Timothy H. Lim
DECADENCE David Weir
DECOLONIZATION Dane Kennedy
DEMENTIA Kathleen Taylor
DEMOCRACY Bernard Crick
DEMOGRAPHY Sarah Harper
DEPRESSION Jan Scott and
    Mary Jane Tacchi
DERRIDA Simon Glendinning
DESCARTES Tom Sorell
DESERTS Nick Middleton
DESIGN John Heskett
DEVELOPMENT Ian Goldin
DEVELOPMENTAL BIOLOGY
    Lewis Wolpert
THE DEVIL Darren Oldridge
DIASPORA Kevin Kenny
CHARLES DICKENS Jenny Hartley

DICTIONARIES Lynda Mugglestone
DINOSAURS David Norman
DIPLOMATIC HISTORY
    Joseph M. Siracusa
DOCUMENTARY FILM
    Patricia Aufderheide
DREAMING J. Allan Hobson
DRUGS Les Iversen
DRUIDS Barry Cunliffe
DYNASTY Jeroen Duindam
DYSLEXIA Margaret J. Snowling
EARLY MUSIC Thomas Forrest Kelly
THE EARTH Martin Redfern
EARTH SYSTEM SCIENCE Tim Lenton
ECOLOGY Jaboury Ghazoul
ECONOMICS Partha Dasgupta
EDUCATION Gary Thomas
EGYPTIAN MYTH Geraldine Pinch
EIGHTEENTH-CENTURY BRITAIN
    Paul Langford
THE ELEMENTS Philip Ball
EMOTION Dylan Evans
EMPIRE Stephen Howe
EMPLOYMENT LAW David Cabrelli
ENERGY SYSTEMS Nick Jenkins
ENGELS Terrell Carver
ENGINEERING David Blockley
THE ENGLISH LANGUAGE
    Simon Horobin
ENGLISH LITERATURE Jonathan Bate
THE ENLIGHTENMENT
    John Robertson
ENTREPRENEURSHIP Paul Westhead
    and Mike Wright
ENVIRONMENTAL ECONOMICS
    Stephen Smith
ENVIRONMENTAL ETHICS
    Robin Attfield
ENVIRONMENTAL LAW
    Elizabeth Fisher
ENVIRONMENTAL POLITICS
    Andrew Dobson
ENZYMES Paul Engel
EPICUREANISM Catherine Wilson
EPIDEMIOLOGY Rodolfo Saracci
ETHICS Simon Blackburn
ETHNOMUSICOLOGY Timothy Rice
THE ETRUSCANS Christopher Smith
EUGENICS Philippa Levine
THE EUROPEAN UNION
    Simon Usherwood and John Pinder

EUROPEAN UNION LAW
    Anthony Arnull
EVANGELICALISM John Stackhouse
EVOLUTION Brian and
    Deborah Charlesworth
EXISTENTIALISM Thomas Flynn
EXPLORATION Stewart A. Weaver
EXTINCTION Paul B. Wignall
THE EYE Michael Land
FAIRY TALE Marina Warner
FAMILY LAW Jonathan Herring
MICHAEL FARADAY Frank A. J. L. James
FASCISM Kevin Passmore
FASHION Rebecca Arnold
FEDERALISM Mark J. Rozell and
    Clyde Wilcox
FEMINISM Margaret Walters
FILM Michael Wood
FILM MUSIC Kathryn Kalinak
FILM NOIR James Naremore
FIRE Andrew C. Scott
THE FIRST WORLD WAR
    Michael Howard
FLUID MECHANICS Eric Lauga
FOLK MUSIC Mark Slobin
FOOD John Krebs
FORENSIC PSYCHOLOGY
    David Canter
FORENSIC SCIENCE Jim Fraser
FORESTS Jaboury Ghazoul
FOSSILS Keith Thomson
FOUCAULT Gary Gutting
THE FOUNDING FATHERS
    R. B. Bernstein
FRACTALS Kenneth Falconer
FREE SPEECH Nigel Warburton
FREE WILL Thomas Pink
FREEMASONRY Andreas Önnerfors
FRENCH LITERATURE John D. Lyons
FRENCH PHILOSOPHY
    Stephen Gaukroger and Knox Peden
THE FRENCH REVOLUTION
    William Doyle
FREUD Anthony Storr
FUNDAMENTALISM Malise Ruthven
FUNGI Nicholas P. Money
THE FUTURE Jennifer M. Gidley
GALAXIES John Gribbin
GALILEO Stillman Drake
GAME THEORY Ken Binmore
GANDHI Bhikhu Parekh

GARDEN HISTORY Gordon Campbell
GENES Jonathan Slack
GENIUS Andrew Robinson
GENOMICS John Archibald
GEOGRAPHY John Matthews and
David Herbert
GEOLOGY Jan Zalasiewicz
GEOMETRY Maciej Dunajski
GEOPHYSICS William Lowrie
GEOPOLITICS Klaus Dodds
GERMAN LITERATURE Nicholas Boyle
GERMAN PHILOSOPHY
Andrew Bowie
THE GHETTO Bryan Cheyette
GLACIATION David J. A. Evans
GLOBAL CATASTROPHES Bill McGuire
GLOBAL ECONOMIC HISTORY
Robert C. Allen
GLOBAL ISLAM Nile Green
GLOBALIZATION Manfred B. Steger
GOD John Bowker
GOETHE Ritchie Robertson
THE GOTHIC Nick Groom
GOVERNANCE Mark Bevir
GRAVITY Timothy Clifton
THE GREAT DEPRESSION AND
THE NEW DEAL
Eric Rauchway
HABEAS CORPUS Amanda Tyler
HABERMAS James Gordon Finlayson
THE HABSBURG EMPIRE
Martyn Rady
HAPPINESS Daniel M. Haybron
THE HARLEM RENAISSANCE
Cheryl A. Wall
THE HEBREW BIBLE AS
LITERATURE Tod Linafelt
HEGEL Peter Singer
HEIDEGGER Michael Inwood
THE HELLENISTIC AGE
Peter Thonemann
HEREDITY John Waller
HERMENEUTICS Jens Zimmermann
HERODOTUS Jennifer T. Roberts
HIEROGLYPHS Penelope Wilson
HINDUISM Kim Knott
HISTORY John H. Arnold
THE HISTORY OF ASTRONOMY
Michael Hoskin
THE HISTORY OF CHEMISTRY
William H. Brock

THE HISTORY OF CHILDHOOD
James Marten
THE HISTORY OF CINEMA
Geoffrey Nowell-Smith
THE HISTORY OF LIFE
Michael Benton
THE HISTORY OF MATHEMATICS
Jacqueline Stedall
THE HISTORY OF MEDICINE
William Bynum
THE HISTORY OF PHYSICS
J. L. Heilbron
THE HISTORY OF POLITICAL
THOUGHT Richard Whatmore
THE HISTORY OF TIME
Leofranc Holford-Strevens
HIV AND AIDS Alan Whiteside
HOBBES Richard Tuck
HOLLYWOOD Peter Decherney
THE HOLY ROMAN EMPIRE
Joachim Whaley
HOME Michael Allen Fox
HOMER Barbara Graziosi
HORMONES Martin Luck
HORROR Darryl Jones
HUMAN ANATOMY
Leslie Klenerman
HUMAN EVOLUTION Bernard Wood
HUMAN PHYSIOLOGY
Jamie A. Davies
HUMAN RESOURCE
MANAGEMENT Adrian Wilkinson
HUMAN RIGHTS Andrew Clapham
HUMANISM Stephen Law
HUME James A. Harris
HUMOUR Noël Carroll
THE ICE AGE Jamie Woodward
IDENTITY Florian Coulmas
IDEOLOGY Michael Freeden
THE IMMUNE SYSTEM
Paul Klenerman
INDIAN CINEMA Ashish Rajadhyaksha
INDIAN PHILOSOPHY Sue Hamilton
THE INDUSTRIAL REVOLUTION
Robert C. Allen
INFECTIOUS DISEASE Marta L. Wayne
and Benjamin M. Bolker
INFINITY Ian Stewart
INFORMATION Luciano Floridi
INNOVATION Mark Dodgson and
David Gann

INSECTS Simon Leather
INTELLECTUAL PROPERTY
    Siva Vaidhyanathan
INTELLIGENCE Ian J. Deary
INTERNATIONAL LAW
    Vaughan Lowe
INTERNATIONAL MIGRATION
    Khalid Koser
INTERNATIONAL RELATIONS
    Christian Reus-Smit
INTERNATIONAL SECURITY
    Christopher S. Browning
IRAN Ali M. Ansari
ISLAM Malise Ruthven
ISLAMIC HISTORY Adam Silverstein
ISLAMIC LAW Mashood A. Baderin
ISOTOPES Rob Ellam
ITALIAN LITERATURE
    Peter Hainsworth and David Robey
HENRY JAMES Susan L. Mizruchi
JESUS Richard Bauckham
JEWISH HISTORY David N. Myers
JEWISH LITERATURE Ilan Stavans
JOURNALISM Ian Hargreaves
JAMES JOYCE Colin MacCabe
JUDAISM Norman Solomon
JUNG Anthony Stevens
KABBALAH Joseph Dan
KAFKA Ritchie Robertson
KANT Roger Scruton
KEYNES Robert Skidelsky
KIERKEGAARD Patrick Gardiner
KNOWLEDGE Jennifer Nagel
THE KORAN Michael Cook
KOREA Michael J. Seth
LAKES Warwick F. Vincent
LANDSCAPE ARCHITECTURE
    Ian H. Thompson
LANDSCAPES AND
    GEOMORPHOLOGY
    Andrew Goudie and Heather Viles
LANGUAGES Stephen R. Anderson
LATE ANTIQUITY Gillian Clark
LAW Raymond Wacks
THE LAWS OF THERMODYNAMICS
    Peter Atkins
LEADERSHIP Keith Grint
LEARNING Mark Haselgrove
LEIBNIZ Maria Rosa Antognazza
C. S. LEWIS James Como
LIBERALISM Michael Freeden

LIGHT Ian Walmsley
LINCOLN Allen C. Guelzo
LINGUISTICS Peter Matthews
LITERARY THEORY Jonathan Culler
LOCKE John Dunn
LOGIC Graham Priest
LOVE Ronald de Sousa
MARTIN LUTHER Scott H. Hendrix
MACHIAVELLI Quentin Skinner
MADNESS Andrew Scull
MAGIC Owen Davies
MAGNA CARTA Nicholas Vincent
MAGNETISM Stephen Blundell
MALTHUS Donald Winch
MAMMALS T. S. Kemp
MANAGEMENT John Hendry
NELSON MANDELA Elleke Boehmer
MAO Delia Davin
MARINE BIOLOGY Philip V. Mladenov
MARKETING
    Kenneth Le Meunier-FitzHugh
THE MARQUIS DE SADE John Phillips
MARTYRDOM Jolyon Mitchell
MARX Peter Singer
MATERIALS Christopher Hall
MATHEMATICAL FINANCE
    Mark H. A. Davis
MATHEMATICS Timothy Gowers
MATTER Geoff Cottrell
THE MAYA Matthew Restall and
    Amara Solari
THE MEANING OF LIFE
    Terry Eagleton
MEASUREMENT David Hand
MEDICAL ETHICS
    Michael Dunn and Tony Hope
MEDICAL LAW Charles Foster
MEDIEVAL BRITAIN John Gillingham
    and Ralph A. Griffiths
MEDIEVAL LITERATURE
    Elaine Treharne
MEDIEVAL PHILOSOPHY
    John Marenbon
MEMORY Jonathan K. Foster
METAPHYSICS Stephen Mumford
METHODISM William J. Abraham
THE MEXICAN REVOLUTION
    Alan Knight
MICROBIOLOGY Nicholas P. Money
MICROECONOMICS Avinash Dixit
MICROSCOPY Terence Allen

THE MIDDLE AGES Miri Rubin
MILITARY JUSTICE Eugene R. Fidell
MILITARY STRATEGY
    Antulio J. Echevarria II
JOHN STUART MILL Gregory Claeys
MINERALS David Vaughan
MIRACLES Yujin Nagasawa
MODERN ARCHITECTURE
    Adam Sharr
MODERN ART David Cottington
MODERN BRAZIL Anthony W. Pereira
MODERN CHINA Rana Mitter
MODERN DRAMA
    Kirsten E. Shepherd-Barr
MODERN FRANCE
    Vanessa R. Schwartz
MODERN INDIA Craig Jeffrey
MODERN IRELAND Senia Pašeta
MODERN ITALY Anna Cento Bull
MODERN JAPAN
    Christopher Goto-Jones
MODERN LATIN AMERICAN
    LITERATURE
    Roberto González Echevarría
MODERN WAR Richard English
MODERNISM Christopher Butler
MOLECULAR BIOLOGY
    Aysha Divan and Janice A. Royds
MOLECULES Philip Ball
MONASTICISM Stephen J. Davis
THE MONGOLS Morris Rossabi
MONTAIGNE William M. Hamlin
MOONS David A. Rothery
MORMONISM
    Richard Lyman Bushman
MOUNTAINS Martin F. Price
MUHAMMAD Jonathan A. C. Brown
MULTICULTURALISM Ali Rattansi
MULTILINGUALISM John C. Maher
MUSIC Nicholas Cook
MUSIC AND TECHNOLOGY
    Mark Katz
MYTH Robert A. Segal
NAPOLEON David Bell
THE NAPOLEONIC WARS
    Mike Rapport
NATIONALISM Steven Grosby
NATIVE AMERICAN LITERATURE
    Sean Teuton
NAVIGATION Jim Bennett

NAZI GERMANY Jane Caplan
NEGOTIATION Carrie Menkel-Meadow
NEOLIBERALISM Manfred B. Steger
    and Ravi K. Roy
NETWORKS Guido Caldarelli
    and Michele Catanzaro
THE NEW TESTAMENT
    Luke Timothy Johnson
THE NEW TESTAMENT AS
    LITERATURE Kyle Keefer
NEWTON Robert Iliffe
NIETZSCHE Michael Tanner
NINETEENTH-CENTURY
    BRITAIN Christopher Harvie and
    H. C. G. Matthew
THE NORMAN CONQUEST
    George Garnett
NORTH AMERICAN INDIANS
    Theda Perdue and
    Michael D. Green
NORTHERN IRELAND
    Marc Mulholland
NOTHING Frank Close
NUCLEAR PHYSICS Frank Close
NUCLEAR POWER Maxwell Irvine
NUCLEAR WEAPONS
    Joseph M. Siracusa
NUMBER THEORY Robin Wilson
NUMBERS Peter M. Higgins
NUTRITION David A. Bender
OBJECTIVITY Stephen Gaukroger
OCEANS Dorrik Stow
THE OLD TESTAMENT
    Michael D. Coogan
THE ORCHESTRA D. Kern Holoman
ORGANIC CHEMISTRY Graham Patrick
ORGANIZATIONS Mary Jo Hatch
ORGANIZED CRIME
    Georgios A. Antonopoulos and
    Georgios Papanicolaou
ORTHODOX CHRISTIANITY
    A. Edward Siecienski
OVID Llewelyn Morgan
PAGANISM Owen Davies
PAKISTAN Pippa Virdee
THE PALESTINIAN-ISRAELI
    CONFLICT Martin Bunton
PANDEMICS Christian W. McMillen
PARTICLE PHYSICS Frank Close
PAUL E. P. Sanders

PEACE Oliver P. Richmond
PENTECOSTALISM William K. Kay
PERCEPTION Brian Rogers
THE PERIODIC TABLE Eric R. Scerri
PHILOSOPHICAL METHOD
    Timothy Williamson
PHILOSOPHY Edward Craig
PHILOSOPHY IN THE ISLAMIC
    WORLD Peter Adamson
PHILOSOPHY OF BIOLOGY
    Samir Okasha
PHILOSOPHY OF LAW
    Raymond Wacks
PHILOSOPHY OF MIND
    Barbara Gail Montero
PHILOSOPHY OF PHYSICS
    David Wallace
PHILOSOPHY OF RELIGION
    Tim Bayne
PHILOSOPHY OF SCIENCE
    Samir Okasha
PHOTOGRAPHY Steve Edwards
PHYSICAL CHEMISTRY Peter Atkins
PHYSICS Sidney Perkowitz
PILGRIMAGE Ian Reader
PLAGUE Paul Slack
PLANETARY SYSTEMS
    Raymond T. Pierrehumbert
PLANETS David A. Rothery
PLANTS Timothy Walker
PLATE TECTONICS Peter Molnar
PLATO Julia Annas
POETRY Bernard O'Donoghue
POLITICAL PHILOSOPHY David Miller
POLITICS Kenneth Minogue
POLYGAMY Sarah M. S. Pearsall
POPULISM Cas Mudde and Cristóbal
    Rovira Kaltwasser
POSTCOLONIALISM Robert Young
POSTMODERNISM
    Christopher Butler
POSTSTRUCTURALISM
    Catherine Belsey
POVERTY Philip N. Jefferson
PREHISTORY Chris Gosden
PRESOCRATIC PHILOSOPHY
    Catherine Osborne
PRIVACY Raymond Wacks
PROBABILITY John Haigh
PROGRESSIVISM Walter Nugent

PROHIBITION W. J. Rorabaugh
PROJECTS Andrew Davies
PROTESTANTISM Mark A. Noll
PSYCHIATRY Tom Burns
PSYCHOANALYSIS Daniel Pick
PSYCHOLOGY Gillian Butler and
    Freda McManus
PSYCHOLOGY OF MUSIC
    Elizabeth Hellmuth Margulis
PSYCHOPATHY Essi Viding
PSYCHOTHERAPY Tom Burns and
    Eva Burns-Lundgren
PUBLIC ADMINISTRATION
    Stella Z. Theodoulou and Ravi K. Roy
PUBLIC HEALTH Virginia Berridge
PURITANISM Francis J. Bremer
THE QUAKERS Pink Dandelion
QUANTUM THEORY
    John Polkinghorne
RACISM Ali Rattansi
RADIOACTIVITY Claudio Tuniz
RASTAFARI Ennis B. Edmonds
READING Belinda Jack
THE REAGAN REVOLUTION Gil Troy
REALITY Jan Westerhoff
RECONSTRUCTION Allen C. Guelzo
THE REFORMATION Peter Marshall
REFUGEES Gil Loescher
RELATIVITY Russell Stannard
RELIGION Thomas A. Tweed
RELIGION IN AMERICA Timothy Beal
THE RENAISSANCE Jerry Brotton
RENAISSANCE ART
    Geraldine A. Johnson
RENEWABLE ENERGY Nick Jelley
REPTILES T.S. Kemp
REVOLUTIONS Jack A. Goldstone
RHETORIC Richard Toye
RISK Baruch Fischhoff and John Kadvany
RITUAL Barry Stephenson
RIVERS Nick Middleton
ROBOTICS Alan Winfield
ROCKS Jan Zalasiewicz
ROMAN BRITAIN Peter Salway
THE ROMAN EMPIRE
    Christopher Kelly
THE ROMAN REPUBLIC
    David M. Gwynn
ROMANTICISM Michael Ferber
ROUSSEAU Robert Wokler

RUSSELL A. C. Grayling
THE RUSSIAN ECONOMY
    Richard Connolly
RUSSIAN HISTORY Geoffrey Hosking
RUSSIAN LITERATURE Catriona Kelly
THE RUSSIAN REVOLUTION
    S. A. Smith
SAINTS Simon Yarrow
SAMURAI Michael Wert
SAVANNAS Peter A. Furley
SCEPTICISM Duncan Pritchard
SCHIZOPHRENIA
    Chris Frith and Eve Johnstone
SCHOPENHAUER
    Christopher Janaway
SCIENCE AND RELIGION
    Thomas Dixon and Adam R. Shapiro
SCIENCE FICTION David Seed
THE SCIENTIFIC REVOLUTION
    Lawrence M. Principe
SCOTLAND Rab Houston
SECULARISM Andrew Copson
SEXUAL SELECTION Marlene Zuk
    and Leigh W. Simmons
SEXUALITY Véronique Mottier
WILLIAM SHAKESPEARE
    Stanley Wells
SHAKESPEARE'S COMEDIES
    Bart van Es
SHAKESPEARE'S SONNETS AND
    POEMS Jonathan F. S. Post
SHAKESPEARE'S TRAGEDIES
    Stanley Wells
GEORGE BERNARD SHAW
    Christopher Wixson
MARY SHELLEY Charlotte Gordon
THE SHORT STORY Andrew Kahn
SIKHISM Eleanor Nesbitt
SILENT FILM Donna Kornhaber
THE SILK ROAD James A. Millward
SLANG Jonathon Green
SLEEP Steven W. Lockley and
    Russell G. Foster
SMELL Matthew Cobb
ADAM SMITH Christopher J. Berry
SOCIAL AND CULTURAL
    ANTHROPOLOGY
    John Monaghan and Peter Just
SOCIAL PSYCHOLOGY Richard J. Crisp
SOCIAL WORK Sally Holland and
    Jonathan Scourfield

SOCIALISM Michael Newman
SOCIOLINGUISTICS John Edwards
SOCIOLOGY Steve Bruce
SOCRATES C. C. W. Taylor
SOFT MATTER Tom McLeish
SOUND Mike Goldsmith
SOUTHEAST ASIA James R. Rush
THE SOVIET UNION Stephen Lovell
THE SPANISH CIVIL WAR
    Helen Graham
SPANISH LITERATURE Jo Labanyi
THE SPARTANS Andrew Bayliss
SPINOZA Roger Scruton
SPIRITUALITY Philip Sheldrake
SPORT Mike Cronin
STARS Andrew King
STATISTICS David J. Hand
STEM CELLS Jonathan Slack
STOICISM Brad Inwood
STRUCTURAL ENGINEERING
    David Blockley
STUART BRITAIN John Morrill
THE SUN Philip Judge
SUPERCONDUCTIVITY
    Stephen Blundell
SUPERSTITION Stuart Vyse
SYMMETRY Ian Stewart
SYNAESTHESIA Julia Simner
SYNTHETIC BIOLOGY Jamie A. Davies
SYSTEMS BIOLOGY Eberhard O. Voit
TAXATION Stephen Smith
TEETH Peter S. Ungar
TELESCOPES Geoff Cottrell
TERRORISM Charles Townshend
THEATRE Marvin Carlson
THEOLOGY David F. Ford
THINKING AND REASONING
    Jonathan St B. T. Evans
THOUGHT Tim Bayne
TIBETAN BUDDHISM
    Matthew T. Kapstein
TIDES David George Bowers and
    Emyr Martyn Roberts
TIME Jenann Ismael
TOCQUEVILLE Harvey C. Mansfield
LEO TOLSTOY Liza Knapp
TOPOLOGY Richard Earl
TRAGEDY Adrian Poole
TRANSLATION Matthew Reynolds
THE TREATY OF VERSAILLES
    Michael S. Neiberg

TRIGONOMETRY
  Glen Van Brummelen
THE TROJAN WAR Eric H. Cline
TRUST Katherine Hawley
THE TUDORS John Guy
TWENTIETH-CENTURY BRITAIN
  Kenneth O. Morgan
TYPOGRAPHY Paul Luna
THE UNITED NATIONS
  Jussi M. Hanhimäki
UNIVERSITIES AND COLLEGES
  David Palfreyman and Paul Temple
THE U.S. CIVIL WAR Louis P. Masur
THE U.S. CONGRESS Donald A. Ritchie
THE U.S. CONSTITUTION
  David J. Bodenhamer
THE U.S. SUPREME COURT
  Linda Greenhouse
UTILITARIANISM Katarzyna de
  Lazari-Radek and Peter Singer
UTOPIANISM Lyman Tower Sargent
VETERINARY SCIENCE James Yeates
THE VIKINGS Julian D. Richards
VIOLENCE Philip Dwyer
THE VIRGIN MARY
  Mary Joan Winn Leith

THE VIRTUES
  Craig A. Boyd and Kevin Timpe
VIRUSES Dorothy H. Crawford
VOLCANOES Michael J. Branney and
  Jan Zalasiewicz
VOLTAIRE Nicholas Cronk
WAR AND RELIGION
  Jolyon Mitchell and Joshua Rey
WAR AND TECHNOLOGY
  Alex Roland
WATER John Finney
WAVES Mike Goldsmith
WEATHER Storm Dunlop
THE WELFARE STATE
  David Garland
WITCHCRAFT Malcolm Gaskill
WITTGENSTEIN A. C. Grayling
WORK Stephen Fineman
WORLD MUSIC Philip Bohlman
THE WORLD TRADE
  ORGANIZATION Amrita Narlikar
WORLD WAR II Gerhard L. Weinberg
WRITING AND SCRIPT
  Andrew Robinson
ZIONISM Michael Stanislawski
ÉMILE ZOLA Brian Nelson

Available soon:

HANNAH ARENDT Dana Villa
MICROBIOMES Angela E. Douglas
NANOTECHNOLOGY Philip Moriarty

ANSELM Thomas Williams
GÖDEL'S THEOREM
  A. W. Moore

For more information visit our website

www.oup.com/vsi/

Charles L. Zelden

THE AMERICAN JUDICIAL SYSTEM

A Very Short Introduction

OXFORD
UNIVERSITY PRESS

OXFORD
UNIVERSITY PRESS

Oxford University Press is a department of the University of Oxford.
It furthers the University's objective of excellence in research, scholarship,
and education by publishing worldwide. Oxford is a registered trade mark of
Oxford University Press in the UK and certain other countries.

Published in the United States of America by Oxford University Press
198 Madison Avenue, New York, NY 10016, United States of America.

© Oxford University Press 2022

All rights reserved. No part of this publication may be reproduced,
stored in a retrieval system, or transmitted, in any form or by any means,
without the prior permission in writing of Oxford University Press,
or as expressly permitted by law, by license, or under terms agreed with
the appropriate reproduction rights organization. Inquiries concerning
reproduction outside the scope of the above should be sent to the
Rights Department, Oxford University Press, at the address above.

You must not circulate this work in any other form
and you must impose this same condition on any acquirer.

Library of Congress Cataloging-in-Publication Data

Names: Zelden, Charles L., 1963- author.
Title: The American judicial system : a very short introduction /
by Charles L. Zelden.
Description: New York : Oxford University Press, 2022. | Series: A very
short introduction | Includes bibliographical references and index.
Identifiers: LCCN 2022018798 (print) | LCCN 2022018799 (ebook) |
ISBN 9780190644918 (paperback) | ISBN 9780190644925 (ebook) |
ISBN 9780190644932 (epub)
Subjects: LCSH: Justice, Administration of—United States. |
Courts—United States. | Judicial process—United States.
Classification: LCC KF8700 .Z45 2022 (print) | LCC KF8700 (ebook) |
DDC 347.73—dc23/eng/20220616
LC record available at https://lccn.loc.gov/2022018798
LC ebook record available at https://lccn.loc.gov/2022018799

1 3 5 7 9 8 6 4 2

Printed in the UK by Ashford Colour Press Ltd, Gosport, Hampshire,
on acid-free paper

Contents

Acknowledgments xvii

List of illustrations xix

Preface: The contours of the American judicial system xxi

1 Structures and jurisdictions 1

2 Roles and functions 16

3 Powers and motivations 33

4 People 48

5 Process 67

6 Politics and policy 85

Afterword 107

References 109

Further reading 113

Index 117

Acknowledgments

The truism that no book is written alone is especially apt in the case of this book. What is presented here is the sum of almost thirty years of teaching the judicial process at the undergraduate level. The general points raised, and the examples given, have grown out of my need to explain the technical world of the law and courts to students who know almost nothing of either. I am grateful to those students. Their questions, incomprehension, and misunderstandings forced me to refine how I viewed and thus taught the judicial system. This book is the beneficiary of those efforts.

I am also grateful to many scholars who helped me along the way. As always, my first thanks must go to my graduate advisor, Harold M. Hyman, who taught me history, the historian's craft, and the law as viewed through that lens. Thanks as well are owed to the judges of the US District Court, Southern District of Texas—living and passed—who trusted me to understand the workings of their court in the writing of my dissertation and first book and whose willingness to correct me when I got it wrong was also very educative.

R. B. Bernstein, Roger K. Newman, Craig Klafter, Josiah Daniel, Vicki Toscano, and Timothy Dixon all read the manuscript at various points in the writing process—in some cases, multiple times. Josiah Daniel, Craig Klafter, and Craig Joyce also provided useful advice about the workings of the judicial system along the way. I am grateful to each for their time and knowledge and, for those who read the manuscript, for their editorial vigor.

Of Nancy Toff and the staff at Oxford University Press, not enough can be said. Nancy not only was patient as I tried (and succeeded!) in stuffing a 100,000-word topic into a 35,000-word casing, but also pushed me (despite my occasional complaints) to do more than just describe the skeleton of the legal system but also explore its physiology. The result is a much better book for the effort.

Thanks are due as well to the OUP blind readers who reviewed and commented on the manuscript. Their insights helped catch some potentially embarrassing factual mistakes and tightened the book's arguments and explanations immeasurably.

I must, as always, thank my family, as they suffered with me during the writing of this book. They are the best.

Finally, I dedicate this book to Brad and Brian Cohen for a lifetime of friendship and brotherhood. NSGs rule.

List of illustrations

1 The judicial pyramid **4**

2 Town Square and historic Lee
County, Texas, courthouse **8**
© miochelmond/Shutterstock,
1405066991

3 Judge Roy Bean Saloon &
Justice Court, Langtry,
Texas, 1900 **12**
Library of Congress, tx0268

4 Traffic court, Washington,
DC, 1925 **18**
Library of Congress, 2016850405

5 Lawyer questions a defendant **22**
Drawing by William Leroy Jacobs,
ca. 1912. Library of Congress,
2010716903

6 George E. C. Hayes, Thurgood
Marshall, and James
M. Nabrit celebrate victory in
Brown v. Board of Education,
May 17, 1954 **39**
AP Photo/File, 17264709679398

7 Poster for Joseph
R. McCarthy's campaign
for circuit judge, 1940 **55**
Wisconsin Historical Society,
WHI-48258

8 One of the first integrated
juries, 1867 **63**
Drawing by James E. Taylor, *Frank
Leslie's Illustrated Magazine*,
November 30, 1867, Library of
Congress, 96513248

9 Judge Pierre Leval gives jury
instructions **80**
Library of Congress, 2016652856

10 "Stonewalled," Pat Oliphant,
1974 **105**
Library of Congress Prints and
Photographs Division, Lot 15351,
no. 74 OLIPHANT
© ANDREWS MCMEEL
SYNDICATION. Reprinted with
permission. All rights reserved.

Preface: The contours of the American judicial system

The American judicial system is important. Courts can have as great an impact on most Americans' lives as, or in some instances greater than, that of the president or Congress, a governor, or a state legislature. This has been so since the founding of the American constitutional system in 1789. Even so, most Americans (let alone non-Americans) do not know about, much less understand, the workings of these courts.

This ignorance is not simply the result of apathy or lack of interest. The American judicial system is complicated, confusing, and frequently opaque in its operations and motivations. It is often hard to understand how courts work and what effects they have, even when people want to comprehend. Unlike most Western nations, the United States does not have a single, unified judicial system. Rather, it has fifty-one separate judicial systems, one for each state and one for the nation (the federal court system, which itself includes two categories of courts: one organized under the authority of Article III of the US Constitution, known as constitutional or Article III courts, and the other organized solely under the lawmaking power of Congress, known as legislative or Article I courts). Each of these fifty-one judicial systems has features unique to it alone, yet each shares common elements with the others, and all of them are interrelated in various ways, so that we can speak in the singular of an American judicial system. Still, the American judicial system made up of these fifty-one court systems is complex and multifaceted.

This book's purpose is to introduce this complex mix of local, state, and federal courts that we call the American judicial system. It focuses on the structures, functions, workloads, and powers of American courts; the politics and laws that shape these courts' judicial functions and their exercise of their powers; and the people who constitute that system's backbone. This book's goal is to explain in simple terms how this complex and diverse mix of people, institutions, and rules combines to give the United States a workable legal system that meets (or, in some cases, does not meet) the needs of the American people for law, order, justice, and dispute resolution.

Underlying this discussion will be a simple question: How can the United States have fifty-one separate legal systems and still be accurately described as having a single judicial system? After all, the differences between the various state court systems and between them and their federal counterparts are notable and extensive. Each court system ostensibly enforces a different set of substantive laws and applies its own legal rules and procedures, although federal courts can and do enforce state laws and vice versa; the specific court structures (number, distribution, and jurisdictions) vary widely; the personnel making up the court systems—in particular, the judges who lead these courts—also vary as to background, method of selection, and terms of service. Nearly every generalization that we make about the American judicial system has an exception; somewhere, some state or federal court does things differently, separating itself from all the rest.

Yet, despite such diversity, in the end there are enough similarities to outweigh the differences. Viewed together, the state and federal judicial systems exhibit several shared themes and functional parallels in their principal structures, tasks, methods, and purposes; viewed more by what they do than by how they do it, American courts are, in fact, reasonably similar. This correspondence should not eclipse the genuine and extensive differences that do exist or the impacts that different substantive laws and procedural rules have on peoples' lives. Nonetheless, these differences are more surface than core.

A first commonality is that the units composing each judicial system are courts of law. Whereas the specific structures in which these institutions operate vary and the rules that they enforce differ, their overall purposes and functions remain the same: the settling of disputes public and private, effectuating transactions agreed to by parties, acting as guardians of private rights and liberties, enforcing societal norms and rules, creating expectations of proper legal and social behaviors, and making and enforcing public policy choices. Similarly, the functional structures of courts (how they are organized, the types of personnel they employ, the jurisdictional divisions sorting courts into different types and categories) generally follow similar patterns across the nation.

A second commonality arises from the limits within which all American courts operate. John Adams, the second president of the United States, declared in his draft of the declaration of rights of the Massachusetts Constitution of 1780 that ours is "a government of laws, and not of men." This truism applies especially to the judicial system. The powers, functions, and applications of courts of law are, by their very nature, bound by the rule of law itself. Specific details may vary from court system to court system, but all courts are limited by the law as to their powers, areas of focus, and methods of operation.

A third commonality has to do with the underlying sources of judicial authority for each of these fifty-one court systems. Though the specifics vary, all courts are the creations of constitutional imperatives and directives. Written constitutions in the fifty states and one Constitution for the nation as a whole set out in varying levels of detail the general outlines of the judicial system: dictating forms, ordaining functions, setting jurisdictions, outlining powers, and delineating the methods by which judges, and other court personnel, are chosen. From this foundation rise substantive laws set by the legislative branch that the courts may consider. Courts also promulgate procedural and evidentiary rules by which courts operate. Last, all courts operate under a set of professional standards and traditions of legal practice shaping their day-to-day operations.

A fourth commonality has to do with judicial impact. Courts affect the lives of millions of Americans. This impact can be direct, as with the roughly 100-plus million Americans who find themselves personally interacting with some form of court services each year, or indirect based on the policy implications of cases usually decided by appellate courts. In either case, courts provide services necessary to the smooth running of the American legal, economic, political, and social systems.

Last, we must account for the political nature of courts. Courts interact with the other branches of government that are political in nature. Courts are consequently affected by political trends— and conversely their rulings and actions will affect politics and policymaking. While these interactions may produce varying results, courts are by nature political players whose actions are integral to the working of our nation's governing process and institutions.

Taken as a whole, the resulting picture of the American judicial system depicts a complicated, multifaceted, interconnected, contested, and important set of institutions working both separately and together to provide law, order, justice, and dispute resolution. The picture at times is not pretty. In many places the results of the American judicial system's efforts fall short of its fundamental aspirations; in other instances, this patchwork of state and federal courts does its job efficiently and effectively, serving the American people well. Yet successful or not, efficient or not, the American judicial system is a significant force in shaping people's everyday lives. Given this fact, understanding the workings and impacts of the American judicial system is essential.

Chapter 1
Structures and jurisdictions

Courts are the foundation of the American judicial system. They are the means by which government helps to resolve disputes between ordinary citizens, between persons and the government, between branches of governments, and between states. Courts uphold social norms. They oversee the uniform application of the laws and rules necessary to the smooth operation of American life. Granted, government also has administrative agencies, which provide administrative means to resolve disputes arising under the rules these agencies make and enforce. But for most Americans, disputes arising under the laws that apply most directly to their daily lives are adjudicated, resolved, or settled in and by courts.

The American judicial system contains many categories of courts. Some courts focus on a single field of law or type of controversy; others are open to a wide range of legal conflicts. Some are limited by geography in terms of what cases they can hear and what impact their rulings will have; other courts have statewide or nationwide caseloads, and their rulings have statewide or nationwide impact. Some focus on the details of disputes brought before them, providing specific remedies to the litigants in a case; others are more concerned with the scope, meaning, and proper use of the law.

Courts also come in many shapes and sizes. Some courts are administrative in nature, providing authoritative notice, judicial guidance, and official validation to matters largely settled outside the courtroom by the litigants themselves; others are trial courts, acting as forums in which to resolve disputes public and private. Some courts serve an enforcement role, upholding public standards and norms or enforcing obligations and effectuate transactions; while still other courts hear appeals from trial courts and thus seek to provide uniformity in the application of the law. Confusingly, many courts combine a number of these functions, while others are limited to one function and only that one function. Even more perplexing, the mix of judicial functions served by specific courts varies by state—in some states judicial enforcement and dispute resolution might be divided between different courts, while in others these powers or functions are combined into a single court.

Adding to the confusion, different judicial systems adopt different naming patterns. Each state is free to name its courts however it wishes. There are some typical naming protocols, but variations exist. For instance, most states name their top court—the court from which there is no appeal (except in specific circumstances to the US Supreme Court)—the *supreme court*. In New York, however, the top court is the New York Court of Appeals, whereas the New York Supreme Court is a statewide mix of trial and appellate-level courts, getting its name from the idea that those courts are the state's highest-ranking trial courts, superior to city courts and county courts. Texas splits its top court into the Texas Supreme Court (which hears only civil cases) and the Texas Court of Criminal Appeals (which handles criminal matters). In Florida, trial courts go by the name *circuit* and intermediate appellate courts have the name *district*. By contrast, in the federal system and in states such as Arkansas and Louisiana, the trial courts are district courts and the appellate courts are denoted courts for a specific circuit. Other common names for trial courts include superior, county, state, trial, municipal, and court of common pleas. Most intermediate appellate courts go by circuit or district or simply appeals court.

Given the wide variations in naming patterns, it is simpler and more efficient, when identifying courts across state and federal jurisdictional lines, to focus on the functions a court serves. When dealing with a single court system, however, it is generally best to simply accept the naming pattern used by that court system.

Categorizing courts by size, focus, and impact

Sorted by function and jurisdiction, we can identify four primary levels or types of courts in the American judicial system: trial courts of limited or specific jurisdiction, trial courts of general jurisdiction, intermediate appellate courts, and appellate courts of last resort. Also present is a fifth category of highly specialized courts that sit out of the normal flow of litigation from lowest court to highest. Viewed collectively, these courts are organized in a rough pyramid shape as to function and the number of cases that they process.

At the lowest or foundational level of the judicial pyramid are trial courts of specific or limited jurisdiction. Such courts are limited by law to adjudicating cases of a single legal topic or focus; in many cases, these courts are further limited to a specific geographic territory such as a city or county. Forty-three states have single-topic courts of this sort.

The most common types of state courts of limited jurisdiction include traffic courts, small claims courts, city and municipal courts, judicial bureaus, and justice of the peace courts. Such courts of limited jurisdiction generally do not hold formal trials with juries, nor, in fact, do they oversee many trials at all. What ties them to other trial courts is that their jobs focus on the enforcement of social norms, procedures, and rules. These tasks

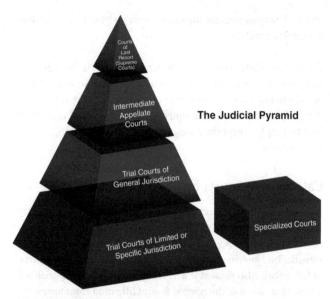

The Judicial Pyramid

1. The judicial pyramid sets out the basic structure of power and authority between different levels of courts in both the federal and the state court systems.

are common to all forms of trial courts, but their methods of achieving these shared goals are different. Given their focus on a single topic, trial courts of limited jurisdiction generally compress the legal process into an efficient routine aimed at processing large numbers of cases quickly.

Take, for example, traffic courts. Most traffic court cases result in guilty pleas. Many defendants do not even bother to attend court but plead guilty and mail in payment for their fines before their first court date. Most of those who do attend still plead guilty; their strategy is to appear in the hope that the judge will reduce their fines compared to what they would have paid by mail. Of those pleading not guilty, most do so in the hope that the arresting officer does not appear in court. When the officer does not appear—a common occurrence—traffic judges normally dismiss the case. When trials do occur, traffic court trials are typically bench trials decided by the judge sitting alone. Most are abbreviated affairs in which testimony is heard only from the arresting officer and the defendant, quickly followed by a ruling by the judge. In consequence, traffic judges generally can process many dozens of cases in a single day.

Trial courts of limited jurisdiction attend to most cases filed in the United States, which explains their focused structures, their emphasis on routine or recurring matters, and their tendency to process cases quickly. In 2013, for instance, limited tier state courts handled over 62 million cases, 66 percent of all incoming trial court caseloads. Over half, in turn, were traffic violations (approximately 39 million cases in total). A 2017 study of twenty states found a similar pattern as traffic violations totaled 3 of 4 state cases filed. In some states, minor criminal matters—misdemeanors in which the maximum punishment is no more than a year in jail and/or a fine of no more than $1,000—are also delegated to trial courts of limited jurisdiction. In 2013, criminal courts of limited jurisdiction processed 13.6 million criminal cases in those states using such courts. Four years later, the total number of criminal cases had fallen to around 10 million, but the 3.5:1 ratio between misdemeanor and felony cases remained the same.

In the federal system, bankruptcy and magistrate courts function as trial courts of specific jurisdiction. Both are deemed subunits of the federal district courts. Each is tasked with specific subject matter jurisdictions: bankruptcy courts for bankruptcy and related matters and magistrate courts for preliminary and administrative subjects such as setting bail or overseeing the first appearances of a criminal defendant. In both cases, the district courts hold formal authority over these matters but refer them to the lesser courts for administrative convenience and expediency.

The next higher level of the judicial pyramid contains trial courts of general jurisdiction—what most people think of as *trial* courts. Courts of general jurisdiction hear a wide array of cases, civil and criminal. It is at this level that jury trials occur and that the facts of a case are judicially determined and effectively set for all further proceedings in that case. Moreover, it is here that litigants have their best chance of having their own needs and wants met. (The higher a litigant goes on the judicial pyramid, the more they will find the court's focus shifting from the specific facts of their case to the proper reach of the applicable law. The result is a somewhat inevitable shift from fact-centered to legal-centered outcomes.)

Like courts of lesser jurisdiction, trial courts of general jurisdiction have various naming and organizational patterns. Most states and the federal system designate these courts as either district or circuit courts; however, some states identify trial courts of general jurisdiction as superior courts or courts of common pleas. Four states—Delaware, Mississippi, New Jersey, and Tennessee—break up their courts of general jurisdiction into two divisions, each with its own rules of procedure and separate judges. One kind hears matters of *law* (generally cases involving property and the resolving of disputes about property or breaches of contract, with the result being the awarding of money damages) and the other of *equity* (cases that involve a civil wrong that needs righting, with the court issuing a judicial order compelling one party to do something or not to do something rather than paying monetary damages). The remaining forty-six states and the federal system combine these two categories of legal powers in a single court.

Though technically all courts of general jurisdiction have the power to hear civil or criminal cases, most states designate some trial courts as criminal courts and others as civil. This designation, however, exists primarily for administrative reasons; in most states, judges in courts of general jurisdiction are permitted to hear either category of dispute. At the federal level, the district courts preside over both civil and criminal cases and exercise both law and equity jurisdiction.

As with courts of lesser jurisdiction, most civil and criminal cases in courts of general jurisdiction are filed in the state courts rather than federal courts. Though state courts of general jurisdiction only processed around 20 percent of all state cases filed in 2017, the total number of cases managed by these courts still topped 15 million. In comparison, civil and criminal cases filed in the US district courts that year totaled only 367,937. Moreover, cases filed do not necessarily equate with trials held. Most cases brought in courts of general jurisdiction never go to trial. Many result in default judgments, summary judgments, or judgments on the pleadings (judgments in which the judge rules, based on the papers of the case, without holding a trial) because of procedural, legal, or evidentiary failings on the part of one or both litigants or because one side failed to show up to argue their side of the case. More commonly, large numbers of cases are settled by the litigants before trial. In fact, the closer a trial is to starting, the more likely it is that the dispute will be settled. A significant number of other cases are redirected to court-mandated mediation and/or arbitration. The result is that a limited number of trials are argued before a judge. At the federal level, of the roughly 307,000 cases filed with the US district courts in 2019, only 2,322 went to trial. Colorado held only 1,700 trials of a total of 216,735 cases terminated in 2014. In Texas, trials (bench or jury) totaled only 14.5 percent of all cases terminated in 2015.

In addition to hearing original cases filed directly with the court, trial courts of general jurisdiction are also typically designated to hear appeals from trial courts of limited jurisdiction. In these instances, the general jurisdiction court does not serve as an appellate court reviewing the application of law by the lower court but hears the matter from the lower court de novo (literally "from the new")—retrying the case without reference to the prior proceedings of the court of limited jurisdiction.

2. In town squares across the country, states built temples to the law—elaborate courthouses that towered above the communities they served—such as the historic Lee County, Texas, courthouse built in 1899.

Most major court cases, civil or criminal, start and end in a trial court of general jurisdiction as litigants generally accept their case's outcomes—won or lost, settled or dismissed. A significant percentage, however, continue to the appellate stage of litigation. Appellate courts review the decisions of lower courts. Their job is to determine if the proceedings below were properly conducted. More specifically, they review lower-court decisions to determine if the law—procedural and substantive—was correctly applied. Hence, appellate courts primarily serve functions defining and enforcing laws. It is their job to determine what the law is (and is not) and to see that the procedural and substantive laws used by lower courts are uniformly applied and enforced.

All states and the federal judicial systems have appellate courts. In ten states with lower population and litigation levels, the appellate courts of last resort serve as the only appellate court; all appeals go to this court for their one and only chance of review. The remaining forty states and the federal system use one or more categories of intermediate appellate courts between the trial courts and the court of last resort.

Intermediate appellate courts exist to filter the appellate process. In most states and the federal system, the losing side in a trial has the privilege to demand appellate review as outlined by statute or constitutional provisions—what is called *appeal by right*. Appellate courts must take up these appeals and review the records from the lower court to ensure that no mistakes of substantive law or legal process occurred at trial. In states with large populations, these mandatory reviews can number in the thousands each year—hundreds of thousands nationwide. Most appeals by right ultimately prove to be without merit—that is, in most cases the appellate court finds that the trial judge did not misapply the law in determining the outcome of a case. Still, it takes time to conduct these reviews to ensure that no mistakes were made; moreover, the pendency of an appeal often creates a new opportunity for the parties to reach a settlement.

Unlike appellate courts of last resort, which generally sit *en banc* (as a single group) to hear cases, intermediate appellate courts generally break up into panels of three randomly selected judges who are assigned to review appeals. Given that most states have multiple intermediate appellate-level courts, there are generally more intermediate appellate court judges than those sitting in the court of last resort. Sitting in panels of just three, intermediate appellate courts, with their greater number of judges, therefore can hear many more cases. The result, despite the substantial number of appeals by right filed with such courts every year, is that these courts successfully process most appeals filed annually—in many years clearing out 100 percent of appeals before them.

For most appeals, intermediate appellate courts—despite their designation as intermediate—are the final courts to review a case.

In 2017, state intermediate appeals courts heard 70 percent of all state appeals filed nationwide, whereas state supreme courts only heard 30 percent (and this number includes cases from those ten states that do not employ intermediate courts of appeals). Thus, seven of ten appeals started, and most ended, in the intermediate court of appeals. The gap is even greater at the federal level. Between April 1, 2018, and March 31, 2019, the eleven regional US circuit courts of appeals heard 47,977 cases. The US Supreme Court, in contrast, currently accepts no more than 80 cases a year, and that number includes appeals from state supreme courts.

All of this means that appellate courts of last resort—which sit at the top of the judicial pyramid—acquire their importance not by volume of cases decided but rather by their exclusivity. Unlike intermediate appellate courts, supreme courts of last resort generally get to choose which cases they hear. This power allows them to select cases that raise matters of serious legal, constitutional, or public concern. Their focus, in other words, is less on the individual case before them and more on the wider legal and constitutional issues raised by the case; courts of last resort thus not only perform rule definition and error enforcement roles in common with intermediate courts of appeals, but also serve an important policymaking function. It is in providing this last function that courts of last resort have their greatest impact.

Finally, there are specialized courts. These are technically courts of limited jurisdiction in that they focus on a single topic or issue of law. What separates them is a combination of their focus and their existence outside the normal hierarchy of the judicial pyramid. Most specialized courts concentrate on highly technical matters requiring specific expertise to process their cases and often hear appeals of matters initially litigated outside the normal court hierarchy (such as reviews of the actions of executive agencies or the military).

At the state level, specialized courts include family law courts, juvenile courts, probate courts, and drug courts. Unlike high-volume courts such as traffic and small-claims courts, these courts put less emphasis on processing large numbers of cases quickly and more on providing specialized services based on expertise in the subject matter. Drug courts, for instance, emphasize the ongoing supervision of those under its authority with the objective of helping these defendants overcome their addictions rather than simply adjudging guilt and imposing sanctions. Probate courts administer the proper distribution of the assets of someone who has died, determining the distribution of assets for those who die intestate (without a will), as well as supervising an executor's overseeing of an estate.

Specialized courts are prominent in the federal judicial system. The typical federal judicial pyramid consists of three levels of Article III or constitutional courts: district courts (trial courts), circuit courts (intermediate appellate courts), and the US Supreme Court (the court of last resort). Yet there are other federal courts that sit parallel with these courts. Most are organized under Congress's lawmaking powers as set out in Article I of the US Constitution; these legislative courts, as they are called, exist to review large numbers of administrative decisions made by executive branch agencies and the US military or to adjudicate large numbers of specialized cases raising technical issues such as those having to do with immigration, patents, or taxes. The courts of the judicial system for the District of Columbia also fall into the Article I category of federal courts.

Jurisdiction

Jurisdiction sets out which disputes a court is empowered to hear and resolve. No court (including the state or the federal supreme courts) has the power to hear every type or category of dispute. For a court to hear a case, two very important matters of

3. Not all courthouses need be palaces to the law; even a tavern will do so long as the basics of a court—judge, jury, lawyers (or advocates)—are in place. Such was the case with Judge Roy Bean's court, held in a saloon in Langtry, Texas, in 1900.

jurisdiction must be present. First, the court in question must have the authority to rule on the subject matter of the case. This rule is especially important with trial courts of limited and specialized jurisdiction, because their very nature is premised on limiting their work to a single type of case or controversy. Second, the court must have jurisdiction over the people involved in the case. Known as personal jurisdiction, this rule requires that a court can exert authority only over individuals or companies that have "sufficient minimal contacts" with the forum state such that the suit "does not offend 'traditional notions of fair play and justice.'" In practice, personal jurisdiction means that state courts can exert their judicial powers only over people who live in that state, who do business in that state, or who committed the act at issue in the given case within that state.

It is the job of a trial court when first presented with a case to determine if it has adequate subject matter and personal jurisdiction to rule in the matter. For subject matter jurisdiction, this question is relatively easy to answer—the issue presented is something the court is either empowered to rule on or not. For personal jurisdiction, the question is more complex. With plaintiffs, personal jurisdiction is automatic: by filing with a particular court, the plaintiff voluntarily agrees to have the court hear the dispute. With defendants, the court must determine how much contact is enough to establish personal jurisdiction. Is a series of visits over a multiyear period sufficient "minimal contacts" to create personal jurisdiction? Is one visit? Is buying goods online from a business chartered in a state grounds for personal jurisdiction? In criminal cases, did the act in dispute take place within the state or somewhere else? Where a court can answer yes to these questions, it can proceed with the case; when the court must answer no, the case must be dismissed for lack of jurisdiction.

Jurisdiction is especially important in determining the scope of authority for federal courts. Unlike state courts, which are deemed to have inherent authority over all matters placed within their subject matter and personal jurisdiction reach, federal courts—up to and including the US Supreme Court—are limited to hearing only those cases involving matters brought under the scope of the US Constitution, the laws and regulations of the United States, treaties to which the United States is a party, disputes between citizens of different states or foreign nations, and suits between states (US Supreme Court only). The first three categories are collectively known as *federal question* suits and the federal courts are deemed to have original and supreme jurisdiction over these cases. The fourth type of jurisdiction is titled diversity jurisdiction, which allows citizens of different states or foreign nations to bring matters of state civil law before a federal court so long as there is a clear separation of state or national citizenship between all plaintiffs and all defendants and the amount in controversy exceeds $75,000. In those instances where the federal courts hear diversity cases, they are required under the *Erie* doctrine to apply the applicable state laws, regulations, and precedents in their decision-making process. Federal courts applying diversity jurisdiction must act as if they are state courts. The fifth type of jurisdiction is an original jurisdiction that may involve a question of constitutional or federal law. Federal courts are deemed to be a neutral forum in which to litigate a dispute involving citizens from differing states, foreign nationals, or disputes between states.

Federal courts also have a unique jurisdictional power known as removal jurisdiction. Normally, a plaintiff gets to choose the forum in which a case will be heard. The act of filing a case with a specific court usually means that this court will adjudicate the case. Under removal jurisdiction, however, a defendant can request that a case filed in a state court be transferred or "removed" to a federal court. Removal is effective upon filing the necessary papers but is subject to remand if inappropriately invoked. In short, a removal will only be sustained for cases that could have been originally filed with the appropriate federal court (the case involves either a federal question or diversity of citizenship).

Finally, the federal courts have limited criminal jurisdiction. They are limited to hearing cases prosecuting federal statutory crimes and ensuring the constitutional protections for the accused. Over the years, Congress has added to the number of federal crimes. As a result, despite their limited jurisdiction in such matters, the federal courts have an extensive criminal law docket.

Federalism

America's federal structure of governance in which authority is split between two independent sources of government power—state and national—inevitably complicates the structures, actions, and powers of America's judicial system. State and federal governments are both sovereign bodies—each holding the right and duty to govern those consigned under their authority. The problem is that these powers and jurisdictions often overlap. For all practical purposes, Americans are simultaneously governed by two self-regulating governments. Each regulates peoples' activities and actions; each imposes rights and responsibilities; each creates and enforces its own set of laws and regulations; and, most important for our purposes, each has its own set of laws, traditions, and institutions.

Yet despite this overlap of laws, institutions, and governing authority, the bifurcated judicial system operates with surprising efficiency. It does so for three reasons. First, there is not a perfect overlap between state and federal laws. Some issues are largely a matter of state concern, while others are exclusively federal. Where this is the case, the existence of two governments for one people does not cause conflict. Each government takes care of its own business and the rulings of the courts of each level of government are determinative for those living in that jurisdiction under those specific laws. Second, where overlap does exist, both sides regularly work hard to minimize conflict. Often, where state courts have initiated legal action, federal courts will defer. The same occurs in the other direction. Courts simply have too much to do and too few resources to do it with to litigate the same matter twice without good reasons. Last, where conflict does exist, federal law and federal courts have preeminence. Under Article VI of the US Constitution, federal law (and, by implication, federal courts) generally has supremacy over state law and institutions where they conflict with the federal. Consequently, where conflicts between state and federal court systems exist, federal courts typically win.

Chapter 2
Roles and functions

Courts are more than mere structures. They are living institutions that act and respond to the public's needs. They provide legal, administrative, and enforcement services. They settle disputes and shape public behaviors. They carry out tasks necessary to the well-being of American public life. If we are to comprehend the American judicial system fully in all its complexities, we must understand exactly what roles and functions these courts provide.

Courts are institutions within which judges identify, process, and apply laws to specific factual situations. Trial courts settle disputes and, in doing so, uphold norms, define statutory and procedural rules, and thus lay out standards of proper behavior. Intermediate appellate courts oversee this process, ensuring uniformity in the application of the laws as applied by trial courts. Appellate courts of last resort reinforce this effort and add a policymaking function as they define the meaning and constitutional reach of the laws and procedures enforced by the courts.

Looked at in greater detail, however, the picture of what courts do becomes complex. Form generally follows function. Therefore, we identify courts across state lines by their jurisdictions and functions rather than by name. Yet the flip side is also true: the functions and roles served by individual courts also are shaped by the specific court structures. The reason that we have four levels of courts, each organized differently, is that the functions of each type of court meet different, and important, needs in society. Although other institutions could provide these services effectively, and in specific instances do so, in the United States we depend on primarily the institution of courts for providing several necessary and essential services on which our society depends to function smoothly and effectively.

Functions

Starting from the bottom up, we can see how the differing functions served by a particular structure of a court build on themselves, much as the judicial pyramid builds from lesser courts to courts of last resort. Trial courts of lesser or specialized jurisdiction, for instance, not only focus on a single topic of law (traffic, family disputes, probate, etc.) but also generally serve a single legal role and function. Many courts of limited jurisdiction, for instance, enforce formal and informal conventions of proper behavior—the "shall" and "shall not" by which society requires people to live their lives to ensure the smooth operation of everyday life.

Consider traffic courts. Cars are dangerous machines. Weighing thousands of pounds, they can cause significant harm to persons and property when misused. Traffic laws seek to minimize these dangers. Limiting speeds, organizing safe crossing patterns for pedestrians and other cars at crossroads, requiring proper notice of a turn or a stop, and ensuring that drivers are physically and mentally fit to drive all mitigate the potential damages if things were to "go wrong." Granted, in most instances things do not go wrong. Driving above the speed limit or turning without flashing one's blinker does not necessarily result in accidents. However, when accidents do occur, they are usually associated with one or more prohibited behaviors. The more the prohibited behaviors vary from the norms set by law (the more one drives above the speed limit, for example), the greater the likelihood that, should

4. Traffic courts, in common with other courts of limited jurisdiction, play an important role in upholding legal standards and practices. In this early (1925) Washington, DC, traffic court, a defendant and police officer are at the bench while other drivers with tickets wait their turn to go before the judge.

an accident occur, the damage will be serious. With this potential harm in mind, traffic courts fine driving behaviors that contravene the accepted norms of safe and legal driving. Their job is not specifically to punish accidents, but to uphold a set of rules that, when followed, limit the likelihood and severity of accidents. The fines are simply a means to this end.

All courts serve to enforce law. What makes enforcement by courts of limited or specialized jurisdiction unique is that when they provide this function, they generally enforce it as their primary—even sole—function. Drug courts, for instance, are designed specifically to enforce societal norms and laws associated with sobriety. Their goal is not principally to punish those who break society's rules about the use of illegal drugs (though, as criminal courts, their process often includes punishment), but rather to find ways to limit and even eliminate such breaches of law in the future. Similarly, city and municipal courts, with their focus on violations of city ordinances and minor criminal matters, emphasize proper rules of behavior in crowded and often contentious urban environments where the failure to abide by such rules could put residents at risk. So, too, juvenile courts emphasize law enforcement, in this instance with a special focus on adapting to the sensitive circumstances, limits, and necessities that arise when children break rules.

Some courts of limited jurisdiction focus more on dispute resolution. This function is most notable in small claims courts. As originally conceived, small claims courts were created to provide a forum for litigants to settle disputes of modest worth without the need for complicated rules of procedure or the expense of attorneys. Though over time the process has become more formalized as small businesses turn to these courts as a means of debt collection and some litigants involve lawyers, the primary goal of such courts remains the resolution of disputes between individuals over small property disputes. Housing courts, where they exist, fill a similar niche for landlord–tenant matters. Family courts also serve a dispute resolution function. However, in this instance, the dispute is over the dissolution of a marriage or child custody matters.

Finally, some courts of limited or specialized jurisdiction fill an administrative function in addition to their dispute resolution role. Probate courts offer an example. In many probate cases, the decisions as to the proper distribution of a deceased's assets have been predetermined by a last will and testament signed by the deceased before death. The court's primary task in such cases is to ascertain the correctness of the procedural filing of the will and then to provide backing to implementation by the will's executor. Only where the deceased dies intestate (that is without a will) or where the validity of the will is challenged by the heirs of the deceased or others does the function of the probate court shift to one of dispute resolution. And even then, once disputes over the estate have been settled or judicially determined by the judge, the court returns to its administrative function supervising the executor's distribution of assets.

Sitting above trial courts of limited or specialized jurisdiction are trial courts of general jurisdiction. As the term *general* in their name implies, these courts do not specialize in a single function but serve multiple roles, many of them simultaneously. These include law enforcement, dispute resolution, administrative oversight, sanctioning powers, and procedural supervision. Though largely similar in form to those of courts of limited jurisdiction, in practical terms these functions carry more weight or real-world consequences. Trial courts of general jurisdiction handle higher-value civil and more serious criminal matters than courts of limited jurisdiction. It is here that trials are most likely to occur and exclusively where jury trials may happen. Trial courts of general jurisdiction are also the courts that establish and formalize the factual legal record for all further proceedings. The result magnifies the impact of general jurisdiction courts.

Consider a typical criminal trial. Criminal trials start with laws passed by the legislative branch. These laws (set out in criminal codes) address unacceptable behaviors and actions that violate societal norms of proper or appropriate conduct. They also impose specific negative consequences for such behaviors—linking specific levels of sanctions to the extent of divergence from accepted norms. Courts of last resort promulgate the procedural and jurisdictional rules under which courts apply criminal laws and sanctions to specific actions and actors—for example, by requiring that proof of wrongdoing by the defendant must be established beyond a reasonable doubt or that prejudicial evidence not directly linked to the purported deviation from the law must be excluded from the trial. With these procedures in hand, criminal trial courts have the specific task of determining the exact deviation of a defendant's action(s) from applicable law as determined under the pertinent legal procedures. The court first determines the facts of the case: establishing the unique elements of the defendant's actions by ascertaining what happened when, where, and how, and to what consequence(s). The court then links these facts to the specific laws that govern such actions and/or negative results. At that point, the judge alone (in a bench trial) or the judge and jury working together (in a jury trial) come to a decision on whether the defendant's unique actions violated the applicable laws as set out by the relevant criminal codes. Where they do, the court imposes punishment; where they do not, the court rules in favor of the defendant, who is said to be acquitted.

Say that homicide was at issue in the criminal trial. The law proscribes that killing another person is wrong except in very specific contexts such as self-defense or by a police officer in the line of duty. The criminal codes explain these specific exceptions, but it is the court's job to determine if these exceptions apply to the specific factual framework of the case before the court based on what a prosecutor pleads and a grand jury indicts. Was the killing self-defense? Did the defendant kill purposefully and knowingly (which would make the killing murder) or in the heat of the moment (which would make the killing manslaughter, a lesser though still serious crime)? It is with these and similar questions in mind that the court hears testimony and evaluates evidence to establish where in the realm of acceptable or unacceptable killing the defendant's actions fall. Where proof beyond a reasonable doubt is found that the defendant did act in contravention of established norms, the court applies appropriate sanctions—up to and including the ultimate sanction of the death penalty (if available)—as set out in criminal codes. If such proof is not found, then the defendant is set free.

Civil trials are different. If trial courts of general jurisdiction in criminal matters serve primarily as agents of law enforcement, in civil cases they frequently combine this law enforcement function with that of dispute resolution and/or administrative oversight.

5. Trials are usually held in courts of general jurisdiction. In this illustration, a lawyer questions a defendant in open court about his personal interactions with the woman in the foreground.

Civil cases, unlike criminal ones, are brought by the purported victim of a wrongful act. Criminal cases are brought by the state on behalf of the general public. The objective here is not primarily to protect society from actions deemed threatening to the well-being of the state or nation, but to compensate the plaintiff for perceived losses or harms caused by the defendant's past or current actions. Civil trial courts, in other words, have not only to determine the relevant laws governing the contested relationship between the plaintiff and defendant, but also to establish by a preponderance of the evidence (50.1 percent) the relative merits of the actions of both litigants. Who, in a contract case, breached the agreement or breached it to the greater extent? Did this purported breach cause harm to the other party? Similarly, in tort cases, the court needs to determine if the intentional or negligent acts of the defendant caused avoidable harm to the plaintiff. In both instances, where the court deems the defendant's actions to have caused a harm to the plaintiff, the court must determine the extent of that harm and ascertain the best way to compensate the plaintiff for his or her losses (identified as damages) and/or to impose orders (usually in the form of an injunction) to ensure that such harm stops. Where the defendant is found blameless of such harm, the case would be dismissed in favor of the defendant.

One common element in both criminal and civil trials is that the courts hearing such cases have the dual duty both to determine the factual context in which the disputed or wrongful act occurred and to apply the relevant legal rules and norms to those unique facts to arrive at a proper legal resolution. This application of legal rules occurs both in determining the proper procedures to be applied in admitting the factual and legal evidence on which the court's decisions will rest and in applying the applicable legal rules in implementing the proper legal resolution(s) of the disputed or wrongful act(s). Ideally, where cases involving similar factual contexts and raising the same legal issues of process and application occur, trial courts within the same legal jurisdiction (i.e., employing the same legal rules and procedures) should produce the same legal results.

This doctrine of common results in similar cases is known as *stare decisis*, which literally means "to stand by things decided." More generally, this rule is labeled as precedent. Courts at all levels are supposed to follow precedent: to deliver similar results within a common jurisdiction where the factual situations in such cases are similar enough to generate the same legal questions. Courts at the lower end of the judicial pyramid are required to follow the binding precedents set by courts higher up on the pyramid. However, with multiple courts operating under the supervision of different judges hearing cases that raise similar but not necessarily identical factual scenarios, determining which are the proper precedents to follow is not always an easy or uniform process. Put simply, different judges can and often will arrive at different conclusions as to the proper reach of existing precedent and thus apply the law in differing ways.

This is where intermediate courts of appeals come in. They are the "cops" of the judicial system, tasked with the job of imparting legal force to *stare decisis* and thus ensuring the uniform application of legal rules and norms across a common jurisdictional landscape. On a more practical level, intermediate appellate courts are the forum to which losing defendants in criminal cases (when the state loses a criminal case, it is generally barred from bringing an appeal of the trial court's decision) and losing plaintiffs or defendants in civil cases challenge the legal rulings of the trial court as inappropriate under existing precedents. This challenge is generally limited to legal rulings, as appellate courts normally do not retry matters of fact. Once a trial court of general jurisdiction has established in the record the factual context in which a criminal or civil dispute occurred, that factual context is set. However, an appellate court may remand a case back to a trial court to secure additional facts, retry facts, or proceed with an erroneously dismissed case. All additional litigation on this matter must be argued within that context (apart from challenges that argue that newly discovered evidence calls the accuracy of the factual record into question—here appellate courts may review the facts in a case).

Still, even when limited to legal challenges alone, the potential grounds for appeals from trial courts of general jurisdiction are extensive. Did the trial judge allow too much or too little evidence of wrongdoing? Were the questions asked by counsel in trial properly stated and on point? Was the jury properly instructed as to how it should do its job and as to what the law required in such matters? Once the jury reached its decision, did the judge properly apply the applicable rules in determining the court's response to the jury's verdict? And, in each of these and similar instances, did the trial judge properly follow the ruling precedents as set by higher courts within the same jurisdiction?

Structurally, intermediate appellate courts therefore have as their primary task error correction. Where these courts determine that trial courts have misapplied the ruling precedents in a dispute, intermediate appellate judges must correct that error—either by reversing outright the ruling below or remanding it to the trial court for rehearing with specific instructions as to the proper application of the legal precedent to the facts of the case in dispute. Where no mistake is found, these courts simply affirm the decision below and the case is concluded.

The objective here is uniformity. A primary use of law is to provide a template for proper legal behavior. It is difficult, if not impossible, to abide by rules of proper legal behavior where such rules are vague or overly flexible. By ensuring that the rules of precedent are applied properly and consistently within a specific jurisdiction, intermediate appellate courts ensure that this legal template not only is upheld but also is made evident to the general public. In this way, the public can abide by such rules of proper behavior without having to involve the courts directly on a case-by-case basis.

Precedent itself is not static. Evolving legal rules and new court rulings constantly shift the ground on which precedent sits: novel factual situations often dictate that established precedents be modified to fit a new factual reality; social or cultural changes can revise perspectives as to the appropriate shape and/or reach of established precedent. Time changes things. So do new technologies and shifting political awareness and values. As chief justice Earl Warren noted in 1954's *Brown v. Board of Education of Topeka*, courts "cannot turn the clock back" to when earlier precedents had been written. Rather judges "must consider [the existing precedent] in the light of its full development and its present place in American life throughout the Nation."

As the first (and normally only) courts to hear challenges to the application of precedent to specific factual scenarios as set in a trial court record, intermediate appellate courts not only enforce existing precedents, but also revise them and even create new precedents. This rule or precedent revision function is inherent in these courts' error correction role. Often, when fixing error, the solution requires a modification of the existing rules and precedents. Recall that the purpose behind legal uniformity is to uphold the effectiveness of the law in safeguarding societies' need for order under the rule of law. Where uniformity of precedent stands in the way of accomplishing this overriding objective, then uniformity must bow to change. Intermediate appellate courts' rulings modifying existing precedent reflect this imperative.

Such was the case when a conservative panel in Texas of the Circuit Courts of Appeal for the Fifth Circuit modified the precedent for affirmative action in university admissions established by the US Supreme Court in *Regents of the University of California v. Bakke* (1977), by invalidating the University of Texas's well-established affirmative action plan to maximize minority access to the university in 1996. Their reasoning: any plan that took race into account in any way was racial discrimination and thus prohibited by the Fourteenth Amendment. A ruling by the US Supreme Court in 2003's *Grutter v. Bollinger* abrogated this logic. But for the seven intervening years, this precedent held force in Texas, Louisiana, and Mississippi.

More recently, in 2020's *United States v. Collazo*, a 6–5 majority on the Ninth Circuit explicitly overturned existing precedent that required proof of criminal intent to distribute methamphetamines as a predicate for "enhanced" sentencing and harsher punishments. Under the majority's new reading of the law, conspiracy to distribute methamphetamines no longer required proof of criminal intent. Merely holding fifty or more grams of the drug at arrest was proof enough to activate the harsher punishments.

This precedent revision function by intermediate appellate judges is important. Except for the ten states that use only a single level of appellate courts, intermediate appellate courts (state or federal) hear most appeals. Consequently, for those appeals that require judicial action beyond mere error correction, the intermediate courts of appeals provide this necessary service—revising existing precedents to fit the novel factual situations or changing societal standards as determined by the trial courts. This process works because, in most cases, previous cases have well established the law's substance. The precedents are clear and their applications well understood, and thus exceptions or revisions to precedents demanding modification are normally limited or narrow in scope. In such situations, there is little need for additional appellate scrutiny.

Yet, what if the needed modifications of precedent are not small? What if different intermediate appellate panels arrive at different interpretations as to how, and to what extent, existing precedents need revision? In such instances, legal and interpretive uniformity demands additional and authoritative resolution. This is where appellate courts of last resort come in. These supreme courts provide definitive answers as to the meaning, scope, and extent of precedent within their jurisdictional boundaries. They establish the ultimate standards for error correction and determine the permissible limits for precedent revision. To quote the words of chief justice John Marshall in *Marbury v. Madison* (1803), their job is to "say what the law is"—and, by implication, what the law is not. The key is that they perform this function in only a small number of cases (around 80 cases per year for the US Supreme Court and a little over 110 cases per year for most state supreme courts).

With near-uniform control of their dockets, empowered to pick the majority of cases they will hear and—more important—to ignore the cases they do not want to hear, courts of last resort can largely limit their caseloads to only those cases that raise unique interpretive problems or those in which different lower courts have arrived at differing conclusions as to the law's meaning and reach. As justice Sandra Day O'Connor noted in a 1988 interview, the US Supreme Court "generally [does] not take the easy cases." Neither do the state supreme courts. Instead, these courts take those cases that raise the most troubling questions of the law's scope and meaning. In so doing, they move beyond mere error correction (though the cases they hear are built around correcting any interpretive errors from the courts below). Rather, they engage in legal public policymaking. By establishing the proper scope and content of constitutional or statutory interpretation, courts of last resort set standards affecting not only the rulings of courts below, but also the future actions of state and federal legislatures and executives.

This policymaking function makes appellate courts of last resort major players in the US governing system. It is they who ultimately decide which social or cultural changes will reshape understandings of constitutions or statutes. It is they who pick which interpretations of existing precedent by courts below will stand and which will be abandoned. And, it is these courts, and largely these courts alone, that get to determine the exact meanings and consequences of the fundamental sources of the rule of law.

oversight by federal agencies and departments. Similar agency structures arose in the states under state law.

Even so, as important as bureaucratic means of administering the economy or social relations became, the judicial system retained a key stake in such matters. In most instances, where administrative agencies failed to provide an acceptable remedy to disputes, agency rules allowed the filing of court cases to bring about a legal resolution. Administrative agencies also adopted many elements of the judicial system in structuring their enforcement efforts. At the federal level, for instance, Article I legislative courts effectively became the federal judicial system's trial courts of specialized jurisdiction. As such, these administrative courts processed large number of cases under the appellate oversight of the more traditional Article III courts of appeals.

Perhaps the greatest overlap between traditional courts and administrative agencies lies in the realm of statutory and constitutional interpretation. At the federal level and in most states, appellate courts exercise oversight over bureaucratic decision-making and regulatory actions. Appeals from administrative agencies' regulatory and quasi-judicial decisions generally go directly to intermediate appellate courts (with subsequent appeals to courts of last resort where necessary). Whereas precedent and interpretive traditions argue for these courts to give preference to the interpretative logic of these agencies, they do not have to do so. Thus, in the end, the judges of these courts decide on the constitutional and statutory adequacy of administrative actions and, with it, the ultimate scope of administrative powers.

While tensions between administrative and judicial oversight of statutory regulation of the basic functions of American government do exist (largely in the realm of statutory interpretation of existing laws and the proper scope of enforcement under these rules), overall the two systems operate in harmony, with each reinforcing the actions of the other. Still, whether through habit, organizational efficiencies, or just the necessities of appellate oversight, traditional courts still effectively dominate the American judicial system. Spread out among four very different types of courts, the roles and functions they serve are key elements in shaping the governing elements of our society and nation.

Chapter 3
Powers and motivations

The decision to turn to the courts for help is never easy. Though formidable institutions, courts have serious limitations on their power and influence. They are prisoners of their docket. Judges cannot initiate litigation on their own; they must deal with the lawsuits that litigants—individuals, businesses, organizations, or the government—bring. Judicial rules and precedents, in turn, often restrict the judiciary's ability to hear every matter brought before them. Fail to show a direct link to a constitutional right or federal law, for instance, and the federal courts have no power to hear your complaint—unless, perhaps, they see a way to invoke diversity jurisdiction. Statutes of limitations and jurisdictional boundaries further limit a court's reach. There are even judicial doctrines that prohibit—or at least counsel against—courts hearing "political questions" or ruling on the legitimacy of judgments made by foreign courts on matters of foreign law.

Even when the courts can hear a particular matter, additional limits to the judiciary's reach and power often make judges extremely cautious in their approach to judicial action. For one thing, judges do not have the authority to make new law. Although they can, and do, reinterpret existing laws in ways unintended when they were originally written, this is not the same as creating a new law out of whole cloth. If the original law is antithetical to change, most likely its reinterpretation also will be contrary to the hopes of those seeking social, legal, or political redress. More important, even if they could make new law on their own initiative, judges have limited resources to enforce their decisions on their own. There are no judicial police (though US marshals do have some enforcement powers over federal judicial orders, their numbers are few and the scope of issues they can enforce strictly limited); judges do not have the power to raise money to pay for reforms by imposing new taxes or fees; they cannot force the general public to abide by their rulings without the help of others. In fact, without the concurrence of the other branches of government—and the support of at least some portion of that general public—courts lack the power to force change. As Alexander Hamilton noted in *Federalist*, no. 78, by their very nature courts have "no influence over either the sword or the purse; no direction either of the strength or of the wealth of the society; and can take no active resolution whatever." In fact, Hamilton explained, "[they] may be truly said to have neither FORCE nor WILL, but merely judgment; and must ultimately depend upon the aid of the executive arm even for the efficacy of [their] judgments."

Courts, in other words, face many institutional and political restrictions on their powers. Unable to promote reform or legal transformation on their own, they are constrained by their nature as courts of law as to the roles they can perform and the results they can produce. Without the assistance of forces and factors external to themselves—litigants, social movements, legislative initiatives, and statutes—courts are severely limited institutions regarding the promotion of legal, social, or economic change.

And yet, as events of the last half of the twentieth and early years of the twenty-first century have shown, despite such limitations, courts can be powerful sources of social, political, economic, and legal transformation. School desegregation, affirmative action on the job and in university admissions, and fair housing rules are just some of the revolutionary changes initiated in part by the judiciary in the last half of the twentieth century. To this list we can add the articulation and protection of a personal right to privacy, the defense of a woman's right to choose (or not choose) to have an abortion, expressions of religious liberties, rulings upholding free speech, expansions of the legal and political rights of corporations, and various protections of the rights of the accused from government intervention.

On a more personal level, courts are equally transformative. For litigants, the actions or inactions of a court can have life-altering consequences. Criminal defendants' freedom—and in some instances their lives—depend on the outcome of criminal court cases. Civil litigants, though they do not face such consequential outcomes, still can have their lives appreciably changed by the judicial resolution of their legal disputes with others.

Put simply, when people get caught up in the American judicial system—whether as litigants, defendants, victims, or just members of society affected by changes in judicial interpretations of the law—the actions or inactions of courts matter. People's lives are changed for good or ill. The world around us is transformed (or, alternately, our place within that world changes).

Jurisdiction and the powers of courts

Not all courts have the same scope for having an impact on people's lives. Courts at the lower levels of the judicial pyramid are generally much more constrained in their actions and hence in the nature of the change(s) they can produce. This constraint is largely because of the makeup of their caseloads. Courts of limited or specific jurisdiction rarely are asked to rule on matters likely to shift the reach of the law or to transform radically the lives of the litigants before them. Such courts—and hence the motivations of their judges—generally focus on meeting the needs of those directly seeking their services.

The scope for impact by courts of general jurisdiction is larger. With their greater range of topics and encompassing more serious matters of concern, these courts have a larger array of opportunities to initiate changes both personal and societal. Consider the personal. Most litigants in a trial are what the legal scholar Marc Galanter calls "one shotters." They do not play for long-term legal goals. They do not want to change the world. They could care less about the evolution of legal doctrine. For a one shotter, the litigation at hand is the most important, even the only, thing of value. Winning (judged by the practical outcome of the specific litigation) is the objective; the scope or shape of the law that affects this outcome is not their concern so long as it returns the desired outcome. This is not to say that one shotters do not recognize the potential of a decision to affect more than just the matter at hand. But future concerns are just that: concerns for future cases or other people; the one shotter wants or needs victory in the here and now too much to be swayed by such abstract considerations.

Of course, some litigants enter trial with the goal of changing the law and thus transforming society. These "repeat players," as Galanter calls them, are individuals or groups who have many occasions to use the courts to further a long-term legal, social, or political objective. Given this long-term outlook, repeat players have "low stakes" in any single litigation; rather, they seek to "play the odds," pursuing in each litigation tactical advantages by which to further their long-range goals. This pragmatic perspective provides the repeat player with several tactical advantages. One advantage is the chance to set up specific legal rules or doctrines that, though they might not provide complete victory in the short run, set the stage for the next legal assault. Another advantage is the experience and expertise that the repeat player amasses from repeated forays into the courts. Having done it before, the repeat player can maneuver confidently, clear as to what strategies will or will not work and capable of using the strategies that work successfully.

The American Judicial System

Trials, in other words, can lead to society-wide changes. Laying out a particularly advantageous fact pattern and challenging or modifying existing precedents in light of this fact pattern set the stage for communal legal change. However, for this process to succeed, the next levels of the judicial pyramid need to get involved. Put simply, if trial courts are the natural home of the one shotter, the appellate courts are where repeat players have their greatest opportunities for success.

The reason is simple. Appellate courts do not regularly deal in questions of fact. Their concern is mainly with the law. Courts higher up in the judicial pyramid consequently have an increasingly greater opportunity to modify the law through judicial interpretation. And policing such modifications—both to hinder change and to promote it—exists at the very heart of the appellate process.

As with other aspects of the judicial system, both levels of appellate courts play a role in shaping this process. Intermediate appellate courts have their primary effects because of the large number of cases that they hear. While in most instances these courts simply uphold existing precedent, in a select number of cases their job as the "precedent police" requires them to expand or contract the scope of legal rules and doctrines. This function of rule or precedent revision may affect only a small percentage of their cases, but given that intermediate appellate courts hear the majority of appealed cases, when they take on this role they transform the reach and scope of the law—at least within the jurisdiction(s) over which they have authority.

A global change to the American legal system, however, requires the intervention of courts of last resort. Given their policymaking function, courts of last resort cannot help but bring legal change. Except for the small number of cases for which they are required to pass judgment (requirements commonly set by the legislative branches of the individual states or by Congress or by constitutional imperatives), the cases that courts of last resort hear regularly raise contested issues of law for which any answer reached by the court resets, or reinforces, legal doctrines, policies, and precedents. Even a decision by the court of last resort to uphold an existing precedent brings change, because the case would not have come before that court had lower courts not previously questioned, challenged, changed, or reaffirmed these precedents in their rulings.

The judges who sit on courts of last resort understand the transformative role that their courts play. They accept that their legal rulings often will have practical implications reaching beyond the legal realm to affect the lives of thousands, if not millions, of people, and even future generations. Such is the burden of their job, especially when these courts are applying their judicial review powers. Judicial review is the power of a court (most notably an appellate court of last resort) to determine the proper scope and meaning of fundamental law as set out in state or federal constitutions—usually by deciding whether a legislative enactment or an executive branch decision is consistent with or clashes with that applicable fundamental law. These written and ratified documents structure governmental authority, distribute power among the various branches of government, place limits on the application of governmental power, and lay out the fundamental aspirations and objectives of our governments. Constitutions are not only the outlines that shape the operations of state and national governments, but also the frameworks within which all governmental action must operate. Judicial review defines the exact nature of this framework.

Rules of judicial procedure

The work of courts affects peoples' lives and transforms our understandings and applications of the rules and procedures that shape our public and private actions and promote an orderly

6. The power of appellate courts is their ability to revise precedent and change long-standing legal policies with a single ruling, as, for example, in 1954's *Brown v. Board of Education*. Here the victorious lawyers, George E. C. Hayes, Thurgood Marshall, and James M. Nabrit, celebrate the court's landmark ruling that in education, "separate but equal" was inherently unequal.

society. But what shapes the application of such powers? What factors beyond court structure and jurisdictional authority and rules (including judicial review) shape judicial decision-making?

Put another way, we know what courts do, but why do they do it the way that they do it?

Our focus here is on the rules, procedures, and legal norms that shape, expand, and restrict judicial action. Courts face many institutional and political constraints on their powers. They are limited by judicial rules, procedures, and precedents that often restrict the judiciary's ability to hear every matter brought before them and that often shape how they rule on such matters.

One important rule is precedent—when to follow it and when it is safe to ignore it. Judges are more than willing to follow precedent. Just as society needs uniformity and continuity in the application of law and legal results to run smoothly, so too do judges. Uniformity and continuity simplify their job; they speed up the decision-making process; and they provide constant standards allowing people to settle their disputes without directly involving the courts in an adjudicative function (which makes a judge's job less overwhelming by lowering the total number of cases that they are expected to resolve). Settling disputes or upholding societal norms and rules is complicated enough without having to come up with new answers to legal or factual questions for each individual case. For this reason, judges follow precedent whenever possible—which in practical terms means in most cases processed by courts of limited jurisdiction, trials held by courts of general jurisdiction, and reviews done by intermediate appellate courts.

But what if the legal question before the court is unique? Changing factual scenarios do occasionally raise new legal dilemmas for which no court within a given jurisdiction has provided an answer. This happened in 1978, for instance, when the US Supreme Court decided the unanswered question of whether local governments were considered "persons" under the Civil Rights Act of 1871 (they were not). Another example arose in Maryland's courts in 2011 when the Maryland Court of Appeals upheld a trial court determination that the use in criminal matters of the new technology of DNA fingerprinting was not a privacy violation where the DNA was "naturally shed." Cases that raise such unique legal questions are known as cases of first impression. A judge hearing a case of first impression has a freer hand in determining the correct legal answer(s). Judges hearing cases of first impression can explore the answers to similar legal dilemmas adopted by other courts outside their particular jurisdiction. Such rulings are not dispositive (they are not precedents); the judge does not have to follow their lead. Still, such rulings can be informative and helpful in guiding the judge toward a proper solution of that case of first impression; judges describe such rulings as having persuasive value rather than the binding value of a precedent. Judges can also draw on their own sense of justice and their preferred philosophies of law, actions they believe to be in the public interest, tradition, customs, social and business usage, and moral standards. Once decided, cases of first impression become precedents and are thereafter followed or reset by other courts within the common jurisdiction, as with any other precedent.

Beyond precedent, courts are also circumscribed by the specific details raised by the cases brought before them. Subject matter and personal jurisdictional rules limit which courts can hear which disputes. Similarly, courts are only supposed to hear genuine cases or controversies involving real disputes over matters of actual substance affecting real people's actual lives. Contrived test cases or friendly disputes brought by litigants who hope to "encourage" a court ruling to shift existing precedent in a desired direction do not meet this case or controversy requirement (such cases are sometimes called collusive lawsuits). While some state constitutions (for example, Massachusetts, Florida, and New Hampshire) allow their courts of last resort to issue advisory opinions answering theoretical questions of law when requested to do so by state legislatures or executives, most states prohibit this practice. The US Constitution specifically bars federal courts from issuing advisory opinions. As chief justice John Jay told president George Washington in August 1793, allowing the federal courts to issue an advisory opinion would violate "the lines of separation drawn by the Constitution between the three departments of the government." If the president wanted legal advice, Jay noted, Washington should seek it from officers within the executive branch. Still, apart from officially requested advisory opinions where allowed, if a case does not involve a dispute between actual litigants with genuine problems raising matters of real substance, then the courts are barred from involving themselves with these matters.

In a similar vein, litigants who bring cases before a court must have standing. This concept means that litigants must be personally involved in the case or controversy before the court. If the court's ruling does not affect their legal status or economic or physical well-being, such litigants are not permitted to bring suit. Without a focused harm, there is no need for a legal remedy. And without a legal remedy to provide, courts have better uses for their time.

Providing the same effect is the doctrine of mootness. Mootness affects cases for which a valid case or controversy exists and the parties have standing, yet for which the courts' rulings would not bring an effective legal resolution to the dispute at hand. In the parlance of the law, cases must be "ripe" for a court to take them up. The court's actions must produce a legal or practical remedy meeting the needs (or demands) of those bringing the cases before the court. Hence, a "green" or "unripe" case is not ready for judicial resolution. In such instances, the court will refuse to hear the matter until it becomes ripe (if ever) for determination. Similarly, if the case has moved past the time during which the court can fix the problem—for example, if a prisoner seeking freedom via a *habeas corpus* (literally "to produce the body") petition has died—the court will declare the case "rotten" or moot and shut down the dispute.

A related limit on the impact of judicial action is the doctrine of *res judicata* (or claim preclusion). *Res judicata* translates as "the matter has been decided." *Res judicata* limits litigants to a single bite of the judicial apple. Once a court of competent jurisdiction has ruled in a particular matter (that is, applied the law to a specific fact pattern), the litigants directly associated with this dispute are bound by the ruling of the initial court hearing the case. Thus, the litigants in the case cannot seek out a second court ruling (from a different jurisdiction that could claim authority over the matter at hand) in the hope that the second ruling would provide a better result. So, too, others directly associated with the same factual events ruled on by the court, who also hold a close personal relationship known as *in privity* with the original litigants, but not directly involved in the initial litigation, also are banned from seeking a new legal ruling when their case is based on the same facts as the original case (what the courts call an *identity of claims*). *Res judicata* does not mean that these other parties affected by the same fact pattern cannot get their day in court. They have every right to bring suit. However, the second court hearing the case brought by these new litigants will be bound under the principle of *bar and merger* to apply the same legal results to the same factual events as determined by the court that first heard the case.

Similar limitations arise from the legal doctrine of abstention. This concept prohibits courts from interfering in the jurisdiction and proceedings of other courts. As with *res judicata*, the idea is to limit litigants' access to the courts to a single instance of litigation. In practice, this limit means that when two or more courts in different jurisdictions have overlapping authority to hear the same case—a situation known as a *conflict of laws*—only one court will adjudicate the matter. When this conflict exists between a state court and a federal court, various rulings by the US Supreme Court on the application of the abstention doctrine generally bar the federal courts from hearing the matter until the state court has acted. And, when the state court's actions are deemed adequate to settle the matter, the federal court will then abstain from action. When the conflict is between two state courts, the issue gets trickier. No doctrinal rule requires a state court to abstain from hearing a case just because another state court has jurisdiction. Each state retains the right to decide what actions its courts will take on its own under its unique laws. However, in practice, most state courts willingly defer action if a court of competent jurisdiction in another state has taken up the matter first. Courts are generally busy enough without engaging in duplicative litigation. Consequently, the first court in which a case is filed generally adjudicates the case.

A limit of a different nature is the concept of immunity. Immunity is an exception to the rule that "a remedy must be provided for every wrong" properly brought before a court. In cases in which immunity is claimed, the trial court is prohibited from action in the name of a wider public good. Take, for example, charitable immunity (which was in full force from the mid-nineteenth century through the 1990s, by which time almost every state in the Union chose to severely limit its reach). Public charities do a lot of good in society. They help the poor, the sick, and the dispossessed. Society depends on the actions of such groups to fill in the gaps of the social safety net. In consequence of this service, many jurisdictions once excluded charities from tort liability. This exclusion meant that, when accidents happened on the property of—or in relation to the work of—a recognized charity, those injured in an accident were prohibited from suing the charity for compensation of their injuries. Even when the cause of the accident could legitimately be placed on the shoulders of the charity, it was protected lest the costs of compensating the injured party take resources away from the charity's important public services.

The law also allows for specific forms of immunity for those participating in the judicial process. Witnesses can be granted immunity from prosecution in return for their testimony in court or before a grand jury investigating a potential crime—even crimes they themselves had participated in. Statutes or executive orders can provide amnesty from prosecution (or, where prosecution has already occurred, amnesty from punishment) for specific groups for acts otherwise deemed criminal. Pardons by state or federal chief executives do the same on an individual basis. Members of the press have a limited immunity (subject to court-ordered exceptions) from having to testify about confidential information or sources. Finally, certain relationships—such as spousal, patient–doctor, client–lawyer, or ministerial—are granted qualified communication and testimonial immunity protecting those in such relationships from having to testify in court about the specific details of confidential interactions.

The most common immunity is sovereign immunity. Originating in the English common law's concept of *rex non potest peccare* (meaning that the "king can do no wrong"), sovereign immunity protects the government and government officials from being sued without the government's express consent to participate in litigation. As with charitable immunity, the justification for this ban on litigation has roots in serving the public good. Governing involves choices; choices made by government agencies or government officials often place specific burdens or costs on individual citizens. While these burdens are real, and the cost to members of the body public may be significant, to allow these individuals to challenge government in their own courts for making specific policy choices undermines the purpose of having government set policy in the first place. Those who govern are supposed to govern for the wider good of the entire public. Holding the government responsible for the costs of these decisions to the few harmed by them undermines the freedom of action necessary for clearheaded and public-oriented decision-making.

Still, applied comprehensively, sovereign immunity can create real costs that cry out for resolution. Recognizing this reality and tired of continuous efforts by injured parties to seek legislative compensation for their personal losses, many states and the federal government chose to adopt standardized rules consenting to being sued in specific instances. At the federal level, this was done via the Federal Tort Claims Act of 1948, which restrained the reach of sovereign immunity by explicitly splitting the business of government between governmental and proprietary functions.

On the one hand, governmental functions include the policymaking aspects of government: when the government and governmental officials are doing the job of managing the public realm on behalf of the general public, actions usually unique to government. These acts remain fully protected from lawsuits under sovereign immunity. Parties injured as a result of such governmental functions simply must accept them as the cost of membership in the wider community or they must seek legislative compensation for their injuries. Even when it can be proven that a government official acted in malicious or bad faith, their actions are protected from civil suit in the name of the public good.

Proprietary functions, on the other hand, occur when government officials are engaged not in policymaking, but in carrying out the many everyday activities of government—tasks like those of private organizations, such as driving a car, entering into contracts, or managing governmental properties. When injuries occur in these instances—car accidents, breaches of contract, personal injuries on government properties—many states and the federal government waive their immunity protections, proactively consenting to being sued in court and to accept the judgments of the courts in such cases as binding.

A last form of immunity is immunity through contract. Often, parties entering a contract will write into the contract provisions immunizing one or all of the parties from liability in specific cases of breach. Other provisions might predetermine the consequences and costs of a particular category of breach. In both instances, so long as the terms agreed on do not contradict any public policies or laws, the courts generally will accede to the contracting parties' predetermined damages. They simply do not have the time to take on disputes for which a reasonable resolution acceptable to the parties is available. However, in a case of contractual immunity, should the judge determine that the agreed-on provisions of the contract in cases of breach produce an unacceptable resolution of the dispute, the judge is empowered to ignore the contract's provisions and impose a different resolution.

A complete list of rules and procedures limiting judicial action goes well past the scope of this Very Short Introduction. Numerous and varying rules shaping the procedures that courts follow exist in every state and the Union as a whole; some are uniform across jurisdictions; others are unique to a specific state or the federal courts. Sometimes absolute in their application and in other instances subject to modification by a judge, these rules and procedures streamline the judicial process. They give the judicial decision-making endeavor a backbone and ensure such important outcomes as uniformity of results, a balance between individual and communal needs and rights, and the prompt application of judicial action and remedies. In a word, they frame the institutional context within which courts operate and judges issue their rulings. Without them, the courts cannot operate with the efficiency and effectiveness that their job demands.

Chapter 4
People

Courts are living institutions. True, they abide by a range of guidelines, rules, procedures, and doctrines—each placed within specific institutional structures—that collectively organize their day-to-day actions and define the scope and outcomes of their work. But courts are more than the sum of their rules and structures. As associate US Supreme Court justice Oliver Wendell Holmes Jr. noted in his 1881 book, *The Common Law*,

> The life of the law has not been logic: it has been experience. The felt necessities of the time, the prevalent moral and political theories, intuitions of public policy, avowed or unconscious, even the prejudices which judges share with their fellow-men, have had a good deal more to do than the syllogism in determining the rules by which men should be governed. The law embodies the story of a nation's development through many centuries, and it cannot be dealt with as if it contained only the axioms and corollaries of a book of mathematics. In order to know what it is, we must know what it has been, and what it tends to become. We must alternately consult history and existing theories of legislation.

Put another way, to fathom the law and the institutions shaping it, we must consider the human element influencing and motivating legal action. To ignore the human element in courts is to misunderstand fundamentally one of the primary forces driving the courts.

So who are these people who operate and manage the courts of the fifty-one judicial systems in America? Where do they come from? What motivates them to become a part of the institutions that we know as courts? And how do they become a part of the court system?

As with every aspect of the American judicial system, the background, composition, and actions of the people who make up the fifty-one court systems in the United States vary widely. At the top are the judges, who vary in their makeup, not only from state to state and state to nation, but also between the differing levels of the judicial pyramid. Equally important, and just as diverse, are the lawyers who argue cases on behalf of their clients, the parties to a case. Then there are the juries, those citizens who render judgments as to matters of fact, and the litigants who bring suit or defend themselves from charges of both civil and criminal wrongdoing. And the circle widens. Witnesses, criminal victims, and the general public all have a role to play in the operation of an effective court system. In a sense, everyone has a potential part to play in the drama of a court proceeding.

Still, some players have bigger roles than others. As with the judicial pyramid, there is a hierarchy of importance and impact when it comes to the people who make up the American judicial system. At the top are the judges. They are the "keystone" in the arch of the law—the one piece stabilizing the entire judicial structure. Whereas litigants bring suits, lawyers present arguments, and juries decide fact, it is the judge who exclusively shapes the application (and thus meaning) of the law. This is especially the case when one moves beyond the trial court level to the appellate court level. Thus, it is fitting to begin our discussion of judicial personnel with judges before moving down the judicial hierarchy to examine lawyers, juries, litigants, witnesses, and finally the general public.

Judges

What makes a judge? What shapes their behavior on the bench and their distinctive application of the rules, norms, and procedures that define and constrain the institution within which they work? The answer is complex. As human beings judges are unique, their actions shaped by a mix of forces and sources common to all but blended differently for each. Still, common factors shape judicial action.

First, there is the personal, professional, and political background of the judge. Who they are as people shapes who they will be as judges. Thus gender, race, religion, and socioeconomic status all play roles in shaping judicial action. So, too, do the personal, familial, and community values that they bring to the job shape how they perform the job. Education and work experiences before becoming a judge also mold the person and thus the jurist. And then there is the intellectual foundation of judging. Different judges have different philosophies and ideologies that form the intellectual lenses through which they see the law. Some judges take a formal, black-letter view of judging; others are more expansive in their view of the job. These choices have consequences. Last, external pressures push on a judge—such as the methods of becoming a judge and the impact of politics on their continued status as a judge. All these factors channel the judge's actions in particular directions.

It is from the unique mix of these factors that the human aspect of judging emerges. And it is these factors that will guide our discussion of judges. To start, how does one become a judge? Again, given the existence of fifty-one separate judicial systems in the United States, the answers vary depending on the location and jurisdiction of the judges.

Article III federal judges are appointed by the president with the "advice and consent of the Senate." As laid out by the Constitution, they serve during good behavior, which in nearly all cases means for life, and their compensation may not be reduced. They can be removed from the bench only via impeachment by the House of Representatives for "treason, bribery, or other high crimes or misdemeanors" and conviction of the same offenses by a two-thirds vote of the Senate. Article III federal judges thus do not have to worry seriously about their continued status as judges once they are appointed to office. The framers of the Constitution adopted this method of selection explicitly to isolate federal judges from politics in their decision-making process.

This judicial independence from politics only comes after appointment, however. The nomination and confirmation of an Article III federal judge is a highly politicized process. Although there are no formal requirements to become an Article III federal judge—no age limits, citizenship requirements, exams to pass, or even the requirement to be a lawyer—the informal requirements are exacting and, normally, highly partisan. In practice, federal judges must be lawyers of high reputation, personally and professionally—able to draw a rating of "qualified," or better yet "well qualified," from the American Bar Association, at least until 2017, when the practice ended. They must be deemed professionally competent and, for appellate judges, ideally though not necessarily have some prior judicial experience. They must also be politically connected. Around 90 percent of federal appointments to the bench are politically active members of the president's party; and when this is not the case, most still will be politically connected to prominent members of that party. There is an old adage that a judge is a lawyer who once knew a politician.

Federal judicial candidates must also want the job. Although publicly campaigning for a judicial appointment is considered disqualifying (as "lacking in judicial temperament"), informal, behind-the-scenes campaigning for a judgeship is both common and necessary. Federal judgeships are highly sought after; as such, there are always more candidates than positions available. One who wants to be a candidate for a federal judicial post must make known his or her interest and present oneself to the nominating president in as attractive a manner as possible. Traditionally, this manner of presentation means holding similar political and legal views as the president and members of his or her party in the Senate, but meeting racial or gender metrics also can be important.

More recently, having a political ideology compatible with that of the appointing president has become an important, even overriding, element in choosing federal judges. Presidents can serve a maximum of only two terms in office. Yet the judges whom they name to the federal bench can serve thirty or more years. This fact makes judicial appointments the longest-lasting impact a president can have on American law, politics, and society. Name enough federal judges, especially justices to the US Supreme Court, and a president's legacy can even outlast his or her lifetime. Thus, contemporary judicial appointments have become flashpoints in the political wars between conservatives and liberals, Republicans and Democrats—major political events fought in a bared-knuckle, win-at-all-costs manner with ramifications that extend beyond the Senate to national politics. This interaction between ideological conviction and judicial staffing has also made Article III federal court judges, already implicitly political players, into explicit participants in the ideological wars of the twenty-first century.

Article I judges are different. Unlike Article III judges, they are not appointed for life and do not require the advice and consent of the Senate for their appointment. Rather, they serve set terms in office—traditionally fifteen years in length—and are hired based on competitive exams or other forms of merit appointment. All this lowers the political elements in Article I judges' appointments. Article I judges are employees who judge; they are not constitutional officers as are their Article III brethren. That stated, they are still judges. They have absolute immunity from liability for their judicial acts, and agency officials cannot interfere with their decision-making. They can also only be removed during their term in office "for good cause" as defined by the Administrative Procedure Act of 1946.

State judges arrive on the bench in several ways. They can be directly appointed by state legislatures or by the governor, elected in partisan or nonpartisan campaigns, or chosen through some form of merit-based, assisted appointment process in which candidates for appointment are first nominated by a nonpartisan commission based on objective criteria and then selected by the governor for service as a judge (with or without legislative approval). Nor do all states use the same selection procedure for each level of court; many choose their trial court judges via one system (primarily elections) and their appellate judges via another (appointments of some sort). Adding to the confusion, many states that appoint judges (especially via a merit-based system) require them to stand for noncompetitive retention elections to keep their seats. Moreover, not all selection methods operate in practice as advertised. Illinois, for instance, is a partisan election state; but in practice most judges enter the bench via appointment by the governor (for appellate judges) or by a judicial council (for trial judges) to an open seat. Only then do they stand for election—running as incumbents.

As confusing as these many election and appointment procedures can seem, several commonalities run through the methods for selecting state judges. For one thing, few state judges serve for life. Unlike the Article III federal system, most state judges serve terms of varying length, most with renewal options via re-election, retention election, or reappointment. Moreover, most state judges—no matter their method of appointment or level of service—must face the voters at some point in their career; many must do so on a regular basis. And whereas nonpartisan and retention elections seek to minimize the role of politics in judicial selection and retention, they cannot fully isolate judges from the influence of politics.

Elections are expensive. Even a retention election can be costly. And this money must come from somewhere. The issue of money opens state judges up to being influenced by special interests (or, at the minimum, to perceptions of undue influence). More important, if the voting public has strong political or partisan views, their voting choices in judicial elections will reflect these views. Consequently, state judges, unlike federal judges, must be at a minimum peripherally aware of political trends in their states and local communities as they serve on the bench—at least if they wish to keep their jobs. This need for political awareness is especially the case for judges at the trial level, where various forms of judicial election are most common and terms of office shortest.

No matter the method of selection adopted or the length and isolation of their terms in office, state and federal judges share many related attributes. For one thing, judges are usually trained lawyers. All judges are college educated; most have attended well-established schools—elite private schools, flagship state programs, or, for local judges, the most prestigious local institutions of higher learning. Most, but not all, have roots in the middle and upper strata of society. Even those judges from disadvantaged backgrounds—based on race, gender, ethnicity, and/or wealth—are usually established members of American society by the time they reach the bench. Further, all judges, to one extent or another, are politically active and connected. One does not become a judge without a power base. This separates them from the crowd. And a judicial seat is earned; all judges are judges because they want to be and recognize the need to show that they are qualified to be judges and merit being named or elected as judges. One does not simply fall into the role of judge: it takes effort (and oftentimes luck) to become and remain a judge.

ELECT
JOSEPH R.

McCARTHY

QUALIFIED BY GENERAL EXPERIENCE

FARM—Born and raised on a dairy farm in Town of Grand Chute, Outagamie County.

LABOR—Worked at common labor for a number of years before becoming lawyer.

BUSINESS—Operated a store at Shiocton, Outagamie County.

LAW—Had wide range of experience as trial lawyer as a member of the firm of Eberlein & McCarthy (formerly Eberlein & Larson).

CIRCUIT JUDGE

LANGLADE, OUTAGAMIE AND SHAWANO COUNTIES

ELECTION APRIL 4th

AUTHORIZED AND PAID FOR BY JOSEPH R. McCARTHY, SHAWANO, WIS.

People

7. Elections are a common method of judicial selection, especially at the lower levels of state court systems. In 1940, thirty-year-old Joseph R. McCarthy, who went on to an infamous career as an anticommunist zealot in the US Senate, started his political career with a successful run for state judge.

Given historical trends affecting economic, social, and political success in the United States, white males have dominated both the state and the federal judiciaries. Over time, women have increased their membership of the state bench to approximately 30 to 40 percent of all judicial seats (depending on the level of court and location); for minorities, the percentages vary but rarely rise above 20 percent of the total (with many states falling significantly below that ratio). At the federal level, gender and racial percentages depend on the appointing president—with Democratic presidents more likely to appoint women and minority judges; only Presidents Obama and Biden, however, named more women and minority judges than they did white males.

Most judges come to the bench either directly from private practice (typically from established law firms), from prosecutors' offices, or from other judicial positions (most commonly moving from lower courts to higher appellate seats). All, no matter their origins, were successful in their pre-judicial careers. Technical competency and professional recognition are unwritten but largely mandatory requirements for becoming a judge. In fact, the higher the position in the judicial pyramid, the more technical legal competency and past examples of professional success are required. This demand for pre-judicial success has traditionally put women and minorities at a disadvantage. In the law as in society in general, women and minorities generally have had fewer financial resources, faced more structural barriers, and have had fewer contacts within the organized legal community on which to build success. Still, viewed over time, there has been notable growth in the diversity of the state and federal benches. In 1980, only 10 women served on state appellate courts of last resort; three decades later, they numbered 116. Similar gains (though in smaller numbers) occurred during these years for minority judges.

Interestingly, one of the more notable changes over time in the makeup of the judiciary has been differences in judicial philosophy between judges. Judicial actions are often shaped as much by an individual's conceptions of the role of judge as by the rules that circumscribe that role. Some judges believe that it is their job to enforce the law as written, to just call (as chief justice John Roberts Jr. put it in his confirmation hearings) "balls and strikes" in applying the law to unique situations in ways that do not modify the law through judicial interpretation. They also believe that anything less than a faithful application of existing law, especially constitutional law, interpreted solely in light of the text of the law as understood when it was originally written, would be judicial overreach. Other judges interpret their roles more instrumentally. They note that, whereas umpires call balls and strikes, every umpire has a different vision of the strike zone. Legal rules, even constitutional provisions, are instruments of policymaking, these judges argue, adding that it is the job of a judge to adapt rules to the needs and challenges of an ever-changing society.

All judges, to one extent or another, shape their actions in response to their own views on the contrasts, conflicts, and tensions between the judicial philosophies of originalism and instrumentalism. That stated, the impact of these debates on judicial action generally increases the higher one sits on the judicial pyramid. Appellate judges focus primarily on the meaning, scope, and reach of the law. As such, it is they who face most directly the tensions posed by the contrasts between originalism and instrumentalism. And, for the judges at the very top of the judicial pyramid, these debates are most important. As policymaking bodies, courts of last resort transform judicial philosophy into judicial precedents and, hence, rules shaping the actions of lower-level judges irrespective of their philosophical views on judicial decision-making. It is here that the personal equation meets the structural elements underlying the judicial process, completing the human forces shaping judicial action.

This brings us back to the main point of this chapter. Ignoring the human element in understanding the actions of judicial actors—in particular judges—gives only a partial picture of the forces motivating the work of American courts. Of course, the opposite is true as well. Overemphasizing the human element and minimizing the institutional constraints under which judges operate give the human element too much sway in shaping our understanding of the American legal system. In the end, it is the almost dialectic interaction of the personal and the institutional that defines who judges are and what they do as judges.

Lawyers

Lawyers have an important, if occasionally misunderstood, function in the American judicial system. If judges are the gears driving the legal process, lawyers are the grease keeping the machinery of justice moving smoothly. In fact, there are few, if any, steps in the judicial process in which lawyers do not play a crucial role. They are the ultimate repeat players who best understand the dynamics of the legal system and thus are most able to navigate its complexities on behalf of their clients. As such, they provide a critical bridge between the clients who demand service from the American legal system and the judges who provide it.

A lawyer's job therefore begins long before the courts ever become involved. For most lawyers, their first and often primary job is to counsel their clients about the likely legal ramifications of the client's actions. Ideally, this is to accomplish their client's objective but keep the client out of court. As one 2006 study noted, most lawyers spend about one-third of their time advising clients about the potential reactions of courts, agencies, or legal opponents. Many lawyers spend the remainder of their time negotiating on their clients' behalf and then drafting documents (such as contracts, wills, and deeds) that comply with the legal dictates. Such lawyers rarely see the inside of a courtroom. In fact, for them, litigation is a sign of their failure to advise their clients adequately and serve their legal needs.

These transactional lawyers, as they are commonly known, make up the largest segment within the legal profession. They run the gamut from well-paid, prestigious lawyers working for some of the largest, most elite law firms in the country, to staff lawyers directly employed by corporations or government, to lawyers working in small law firms or as solo practitioners providing general legal services. Collectively, these lawyers shape what could be called the hidden docket of the American judicial system—the myriad legal transactions that keep our economy and society moving smoothly and efficiently without the need for direct action on the part of the courts or other agencies of the government. Without these largely unseen services, the formal legal structures of the nation soon would be overwhelmed and, inevitably, collapse from the weight of the demands placed on them.

Then there are those lawyers who do go to court. As with transactional lawyers, these litigators run the gamut from elite lawyers who specialize in one form or another of corporate or appellate litigation, to government prosecutors and public defenders who serve the public in court, to private practitioners in small firms or in solo practice who generally specialize either as plaintiffs' or defense attorneys in civil cases or as defense attorneys in criminal matters. As with transactional attorneys, litigators also spend a portion of their time and effort counseling clients, only here their objective is less how to avoid litigation than how to maximize the likelihood of success in the litigation process. Litigators also engage in investigation and/or research on behalf of their clients as they strive for victory in court.

Perhaps the most important function of litigators is that of negotiator. Trials are costly and time-consuming, and the results are uncertain. Consequently, the best outcome in most litigations is to settle the case without going to trial or, in criminal cases, to negotiate plea bargains that fix the outcome of a criminal case without going to trial. Plea bargaining is, in fact, an essential tool in the smooth operation of the criminal court system. Too many defendants are brought into the criminal justice system every year for every case to go to a full trial. To move cases through the system as efficiently as possible, defense lawyers and prosecutors engage in negotiations to trade guilty pleas to lesser charges for reduced sentences, to remove tangential charges (such as not prosecuting all possible charges against a defendant), or to consolidate differing but related criminal cases and thus to lower the length of jail sentences or probationary terms. The result is that more than 90 percent of criminal cases at both the state and the federal level end in some form of plea bargain.

Lawyers are not only important to the efficient operation of the judicial system; they also make up one of the largest components of this system. As of November 2020, the American Bar Association estimated that a total of 1.33 million licensed, active attorneys work in the United States. Each year, US law schools add an additional 30,000 to 35,000 new lawyers to the mix. These numbers compare tellingly with the numbers of new lawyers in Japan, which adds only about 350 to 400 attorneys to active practice each year. One reason for such disparities is that many of the functions filled by transactional lawyers in the United States could be, and are, filled by nonlawyers in other countries.

One effect of this situation—like that of the makeup of judges—is that the legal profession is divided not just by function (transactional lawyer vs. litigator) but also by status. Some legal roles have higher status and compensation than others. Generally, entry into these more lucrative positions goes to those who already have a higher status within society and the profession. In the case of lawyers, this determination of status is often dependent on the law school one attends and the recognition that one achieves within the law school environment. There have been growing numbers of women and minorities entering the legal profession in recent years, but the leadership of the bar has so far remained predominantly white and male.

Jurors

For the average citizen, entry into the American judicial system comes in one of four ways: as a juror, a litigant, a witness, or a bystander or victim affected by a legal ruling or action. The most active of these roles is that of a juror. Though most court cases are settled by the parties without the involvement of a jury, a small but still significant number of cases do go the full jury trial route. When such a case goes to trial, jurors play their very important role.

A jury (technically a *petit* or small jury) consists of a group of citizens serving as jurors (averaging in number somewhere between six and twelve members, depending on the jurisdiction). They are brought to the courthouse specifically to determine the weight or significance given to the how, what, when, and where of a civil or criminal dispute—in other words, to determine the importance of specific factual elements necessary to dispose of or reconcile the differences in dispute in a trial. A jury trial formally begins with jury selection, or *voir dire* (literally "to see to say," or more colloquially, "to speak the truth"). Drawing on a pool of randomly selected citizens from within the court's jurisdiction, usually consisting of double or treble the actual number of jurors required to decide the case (but growing as large as needed to pick a final jury panel), the *voir dire* process begins with the assumption that all members of the jury pool are qualified to serve on the jury. That is to say, the members of the jury pool are assumed to be the jury. What *voir dire* does is remove selectively members of the jury pool from consideration until the final jury panel is assembled.

This essentially negative process allows potential jurors to be removed for only two possible reasons. The first is for cause. Jurors who have preexisting knowledge or opinions about the case, who are personally acquainted with the litigants or attorneys, or who hold views prejudicial to one or the other side in the dispute are deemed inappropriate jury members and will be excused. To determine if these conditions for removal exist, *voir dire* consists of a process in which the lawyers for each side ask each potential juror a set of questions. Based on their answers, the lawyer for either side can object to a specific juror's inclusion in the final jury panel. Lawyers are normally allowed unlimited removals for cause. So long as they can convince the judge that a potential juror is unsuitable for this jury, they can exclude that juror.

In addition to removal for cause, lawyers on both sides have a limited number of peremptory challenges. These are "free" removals for which no reason for removal need be provided. The only limit is that peremptory challenges cannot be used to exclude jurors based solely or primarily on their race, religion, ethnicity, or gender. Given their limited number, peremptory challenges are a scarce resource; once a lawyer has used up his or her peremptory challenges, he or she must accept all subsequent jurors who cannot be removed for cause.

The *voir dire* process continues until all jurors who could be removed for cause have been and until all the peremptory challenges available to the lawyers have been either used or waived. At this point, the jury's role becomes passive. Their job during the trial is to sit and listen. They are not permitted to talk about the case, even among themselves, until the trial has concluded. Only after both sides have rested their case and the judge (with the advice of both counsels) has instructed the jury as to their job and the dictates of the law can the jury actively engage with the case before it.

It is at this stage that the jury becomes the central player in the litigation. Having (hopefully) absorbed all the information provided at trial, and guided by the judge's instructions, the jury has the important job of determining the unique factual context of the case at hand. It is the jurors who decide which witnesses to

8. In 1867, a lawyer argues his case to one of the first integrated juries in American history.

believe, which documents are relevant, and ultimately which facts when applied to the legal rules outlined by the judge are determinative in deciding the outcome of the case. In civil cases, the jurors must determine which side made the stronger, more persuasive argument on the case and its proper outcome. In criminal cases, the jurors decide whether the state has proven beyond a reasonable doubt that the defendant is guilty of the crimes charged.

Being a juror can be confusing. Every day, citizens with no legal training are asked to evaluate factual evidence and testimony in a context shaped by the judge's instructions as to the reach and meaning of the law, to reach a conclusion as to which side is right and which side is wrong (in a civil case) or who is guilty or not (in a criminal matter). This is not easy. Yet, most jurors take their job seriously and seek to do the best they can to arrive at the proper resolution of the civil dispute or criminal case.

Litigants

Litigants have a special place in the judicial process. In one sense, a court case is all about them. It is their dispute or their freedom that is the whole point of the proceedings. Without litigants, there would be no need for the courts to get involved. That stated, litigants have a relatively minor role to play in the process of litigation. Their main job is to hire a lawyer, work with the lawyer to set out a legal strategy for the case (which the lawyer then pursues), and—when a settlement or plea bargain is on the table—decide whether to accept it or not. That is about it in most litigation. Of course, the few decisions a litigant must make in this situation are very important. Picking the right lawyer, deciding on the desired outcomes in a case, and making the final call on a settlement or plea bargain are key elements in shaping the outcome of litigation.

As for criminal defendants, the biggest difference between their experience and that of a civil litigant has to do with two factors: the potential consequences of losing and the rules that shape the legal process before and during trial. In a criminal trial, the defendant faces the prospect of losing his or her freedom: of facing financial penalties, jail or prison time, intrusive probation, or, in the ultimate sanction, the loss of life. In compensation, criminal defendants have additional constitutional protections not always available to civil litigants. As currently applied, the majority of the Bill of Rights (as incorporated or imposed on the states via the Fourteenth Amendment) and the Fourteenth Amendment itself provides a guarantee of due process of law ensuring a fair trial: equal protection of the laws guaranteeing equal treatment based on race, ethnicity, and religion; the right to legal counsel (even if a criminal defendant cannot afford it) at all significant stages of a criminal prosecution; protections from illegal search and seizure; the right to confront witnesses; the right to a jury trial (in federal courts only); the right to a speedy trial; and the right not to incriminate oneself. Criminal defendants are also protected from cruel and unusual punishment upon conviction; further, under double jeopardy rules, a defendant can be tried only once for the same crime.

Victims, witnesses, and the general public

Finally, there is everybody else: victims, witnesses, and the general public affected by the outcome of the litigation process. Often the forgotten participants in a trial, victims and witnesses play an important, but very narrow, role in the litigation process. One would think that the victim of a crime would be the central player in a criminal case, but this frequently is not the case. The state brings criminal cases against defendants for their crimes against the community. The victim is merely "evidence" of this wrong. This fact does not mean that prosecutors will not seek out the preferences and opinions of victims of a crime as regard plea bargains and charging decisions, but this communication is mostly a courtesy. The wronged party in a criminal case is the people, and it is their need for security and stability that ultimately shapes a prosecutor's actions. As for witnesses, while their participation in a trial is essential to the litigation process, they have no role or function beyond communicating their direct knowledge of the matters in dispute; if they did not see or hear something directly, they cannot testify to it in court. The only exceptions to this definition of the witness's role are expert witnesses certified by the court as experts in a topic and thus permitted to express their opinion to the jury.

Then there are the rest of us. In a very real sense, the most important impact of a trial is not on the direct participants, but on society. As noted previously, most legal work in America involves trying to stay out of court. It is through the rulings of courts in individual cases that lawyers can piece together the standards of proper legal behavior to advise their clients on how to avoid breaking the law or how to avoid a dispute leading to civil litigation. So too for everyone else. The judicial process helps to shape the "good and bad," the "should and should not," the "legal and illegal" standards by which we, as members of society, live our lives.

Chapter 5
Process

Most Americans find themselves directly caught up in the American judicial system in one of four ways. They can be called for jury duty, they can be crime victims, they can be litigants in a civil dispute, or they can be defendants in a criminal case.

Being a criminal defendant or a civil litigant is the most intense contact that an individual who is not a lawyer or judge is likely to have with a state or federal court. Here the stakes are highest; here the outcomes can affect the individual the most; and here the process is most confusing to nonexperts. A trial includes many complex interactions, decisions, and processes. The steps and stages of either a criminal charge or a civil dispute have many moving parts, all impinging on the case's outcome. Confusion about the steps and processes through which a case progresses in the legal system thus can have negative, even tragic, consequences.

Civil disputes

We begin with civil cases. A civil dispute starts with a triggering event. This event could be anything from an automobile or industrial accident to a breach of contract, from a dispute over property to a petition for divorce. In fact, any noncriminal conflict in which two or more parties find themselves at odds as to the proper resolution and for which judicial action can provide a remedy can be a triggering event for a civil case. The key elements necessary are the event's noncriminal nature, its character as a dispute, and its being subject to judicial resolution.

Our example will center on a tort (a noncontractual civil wrong) in the form of a slip and fall on a slick sidewalk (what is colloquially called a personal injury case). The case begins when the victim of the fall—call her Jane—decides that the cause of the fall rests with her neighbor Dan, the owner of the sidewalk on which she fell, because of his negligent actions; further, given this fault asserted against Dan, Jane believes that she is entitled to compensation from him for her physical, financial, and emotional losses—including an injured back, a broken arm, extensive medical bills, and lost income in the weeks during which she was unable to work.

Having decided to act, Jane's first step is to seek legal advice. It is possible that she is incorrect in her belief that compensation is legally due her for her injuries or, alternatively, that what compensation she is likely to receive might be so small as to make bringing her case to the courts a waste of her and her lawyer's time and resources. As the ultimate repeat player in the legal system, a lawyer is best situated to give Jane sound advice as to her options.

Often, these initial or exploratory conversations with an attorney are done gratis (for free) on the part of the lawyer. By not charging a fee for this first meeting, the lawyer can attract potential paying clients. Lawyers, as much as the injured party, are seeking to determine if a valid case or controversy exists and if the potential return on the case warrants their time and effort in filing, pursuing, and arguing the claim. At this point, no contractual relationship exists between the lawyer and the litigant. They are just talking. Should the lawyer decide that Jane lacks a valid or likely unsuccessful case, both sides can walk away with no cost or obligation to either side (though, even after a preliminary consultation, a lawyer is bound by a duty of confidentiality as to matters disclosed by the client). Even if the lawyer chooses to charge for this first meeting (and in contractual matters, lawyers often do), no legal obligations exist other than for the litigant to pay for the lawyer's time. Jane is free to listen to what the lawyer has to say, but she also need not hire the lawyer to actually file a lawsuit.

Still, given that the litigant is interested in the possibility of suing and that the lawyer makes her living by filing lawsuits, both sides have an interest in working together should the lawyer determine that Jane has a valid and potentially successful claim to bring. It is at this point that both the injured party and the lawyer begin to talk seriously about the elements of their impending contractual relationship and the litigation that will follow.

The lawyer begins by setting out the terms by which she will be paid for her labor. Four possibilities exist. Jane could pay a fixed fee for the entirety of the litigation, pay the lawyer by the hour, pay the lawyer a retainer for legal services over a set period, or enter into a contingency fee arrangement. Contingency fees—the method of payment most common in personal injury suits such as Jane's—mean that the lawyer takes no money up front; in fact, the lawyer agrees to cover all costs of the litigation. Should the case be brought to a successful conclusion and Jane receives compensation for her losses, the lawyer would take a percentage of a court's award (or negotiated settlement) as her fee. The percentage owed to the lawyer varies from state to state, but personal injury cases are typically restricted to a maximum of 40 percent of the award if the case is settled out of court; the fee is more if the case goes to trial. In essence, the lawyer is gambling that 40 percent or more of Jane's compensation will be larger than the net of the lawyer's costs and time in arguing the case. Jane, in turn, gives up 40 percent or more of her award in return for not having to cover the costs of bringing suit if the case is lost.

At this stage, the courts are not yet involved in Jane's dispute with Dan. In fact, with knowledge of how the courts are likely to act, Jane's lawyer is likely to get in touch with Dan (and, as soon as he hires one, his lawyer) to discuss a possible settlement based on those expectations. Should Dan have homeowner's insurance, his lawyer will give notice of a potential claim to the insurance company, which would also become involved in these negotiations. (Though it would usually not become a named party in a subsequent lawsuit, the insurance company has a financial stake in the outcome of this case because of its contract to insure Dan against such claims and thus a key role to play in settlement discussions.) Settling the dispute before involving the courts minimizes costs for all concerned. Jane gets her compensation more quickly, her lawyer makes more profit, and Dan and his insurance company are saved the legal costs of defending against Jane's demands for compensation through potentially lengthy, and expensive, court proceedings. Should a settlement be worked out, the dispute is over.

Large numbers of civil disputes begin and end in this manner. Litigation is an expensive and slow process, the results if a jury is involved are often unpredictable, and the outcome in terms of compensation is chancy at best for both parties. Still, not all disputes can be settled informally based on expectations of how a court might respond. To the defendant's eyes, Jane may be asking for too much compensation, or Dan may question the legitimacy of Jane's claims. Should Dan's property be a business, he might want to fight against Jane's claims for fear of setting a legal precedent that would encourage similar suits against his business. Or Dan may just be a contentious individual determined to fight the suit whatever the eventual outcome. Whatever the reason, if Jane's lawyer's settlement request is turned down or ignored, her next step is to involve the courts by launching her lawsuit.

She commences her case by filing a complaint with a court of competent jurisdiction holding both subject matter and personal authority over both parties. Where more than one court fits this description—and under conflict of laws doctrines, this is often the case—Jane's lawyer is free to choose which court of competent jurisdiction to file in. Customarily, the plaintiff's choice of a court will be based on her lawyer's estimation of which court offers the best chance of legal victory. Where there is a choice, this search for the court most likely to rule in the plaintiff's favor is known as forum shopping. In Jane's case, however, the choice of court is likely limited to the local trial court of general jurisdiction.

A complaint consists of three elements. First, it identifies the defendant(s). Second, it lays out the facts of the case as understood by the plaintiff and lists the nature of the claims being made against the defendant rooted in those facts. Third, the complaint provides a prayer for relief delineating exactly what remedies the plaintiff seeks from the court.

Possible remedies fall into two categories. The first are common law remedies in which the goal is to reimburse the plaintiff via compensatory damages for past and current losses caused by the defendant. These losses can be both specific monetary losses in the form of medical bills, time off from work as a result of injury, or losses as the result of a contract breach, and nonmonetary losses such as pain and suffering. In both cases, the plaintiff is not supposed to profit from this compensation. The goal in compensatory damages is to place the plaintiff back in the position that she would have been in had the defendant not caused harm to the plaintiff in the first place (substituting money for nonmonetary harms as appropriate). When the plaintiff's actions are both intentional and egregious, courts can also assign punitive damages (usually assessed at a multiple of the amount of compensatory damages) as a form of punishment and as a warning to other potential plaintiffs not to act in this manner.

The second form of remedies are equitable remedies, which concentrate on shaping the present and future actions of the defendant—most commonly via an injunction prohibiting or requiring some specific act by the defendant—such that the harm suffered by the plaintiff ends and/or the relative standing of both parties is reset to a condition like that which would have existed had no wrongful act occurred.

In Jane's case, neither punitive damages nor equitable remedies would be an appropriate resolution because the defendant's harmful actions (negligently allowing his sidewalk to become slick enough to cause Jane's slip and fall) were neither intentional nor egregious, though they might be ongoing. Thus, her complaint likely would request only compensatory damages.

Having filed the complaint with the court, Jane's lawyer would request issuance of a summons from the clerk of the court to be delivered to the defendant by either a sheriff's deputy or a private process server (depending on the rules and procedures of the court). The summons consists of an official notice identifying both the court in which the case has been filed and the plaintiff filing the complaint and designating a specific deadline by which the defendant must respond to the complaint or face a default judgment (a judgment by the court based only on the plaintiff's filings). Service of the summons can be made in person (handed directly to the defendant), to a resident of the defendant's home (usually someone over the age of fourteen), or in some jurisdictions by certified or regular mail. Should none of these methods succeed, the courts allow constructive service— publishing notice of the summons in a journal of record (a publication in which such summons are normally printed) over a multiweek period.

Having been summoned, the defendant has to file a response, but he has a choice to make. Dan can challenge the complaint. His attorney can file a motion to dismiss, arguing that the court lacks jurisdiction over this matter or that the summons was inadequate. He can also challenge elements of the complaint, asking the court to dismiss the entire complaint or certain portions of it because the allegations fail to state a claim on which the court could grant relief, or he could seek to strike any scandalous, immaterial, or irrelevant matters. Or Dan can choose to defend the merits of the case before this court by filing an answer. An answer is a direct response to the complaint. In it, the defendant can admit to the truth of certain facts (which therefore would not have to be argued at trial), deny other facts or contentions, generally defend himself against the plaintiff's claims and arguments, and even make a counterclaim against the plaintiff, contending that he, and not the plaintiff, deserves the court's remedial relief.

Once the answer is filed, Jane as the plaintiff has the right to file an amended complaint responding to the defensive arguments made by the defendant in the answer. In some cases, this revised complaint might require an amended answer, which produces a second amended complaint followed by a second amended answer, and so on. The point of all this pleading, as it is called, is to narrow the factual and legal issues before the court. If both sides agree to certain facts, there is no need to prove them at trial; also, if they can agree that certain legal questions are not relevant to the case, they can be excluded from the oral argument. In some instances, one or both parties can file a motion for summary judgment, arguing that, because there are no material factual disputes between the parties based on the pleadings and undisputed evidence filed with the motion, there is no need for a trial to determine the facts of the case; the judge could go straight to determining answers to the legal questions that divide the two sides and render judgment.

In most instances, although the pleadings and motions operate to narrow the scope of the dispute, they do not resolve all controversies and the court is obliged to schedule the case for trial. Such would likely be the case for Jane's suit. If the parties could not reach agreement on the relevant facts and legal responsibilities before involving the court—the question whether

Dan was negligent in maintaining the sidewalk—they are unlikely to do so early in the litigation process. But, as the case progresses toward trial and judgment, the incentives to compromise and avoid the costs and uncertainty of a trial will increase. Many cases that could not be settled before involving the courts are resolved in the weeks, days, or even minutes before the trial begins (the so-called courthouse steps settlement).

The date set for trial can vary widely depending on how busy the court is. In crowded urban areas and in most federal district courts, dockets are congested and cases can require years before a trial. Even if the court is not excessively busy, the date set for a trial will normally be many months or even a year in the future. Such time is needed because several key steps must be accomplished between the last of the pleadings and the beginning of the trial.

The most important of these intermediate steps is discovery. Discovery is a process in which both sides in a dispute obtain and examine information (or evidence) possessed by the other side. Discovery is done by providing the identity and location of persons associated with the case, affording access to these individuals for questioning either through written interrogatories (questions) or live depositions (interviews taken before and transcribed by a court reporter), facilitating the transfer of documents germane to the case, disclosing the identity and opinions of experts likely to be asked to testify at trial, responding to requests for admissions or denials of specific facts associated with the case (to create a factual record before the trial), and permitting physical and mental examinations of parties to the suit.

This transfer of knowledge and information is important. Trials are supposed to be conducted fairly, based on an examination of the relevant evidence by the "trier of fact," whether the judge of the court or a jury. Surprise witnesses, trickery, and deceit in the form of hidden information are not allowed to determine the victor in a lawsuit. Discovery facilitates this process.

This said, important limits are built into the discovery process. All requests for disclosure of information by the parties must be reasonably calculated to lead to the discovery of information relevant to the case at hand. Neither side can engage in "fishing" expeditions that dig through the opposition's records or witnesses in a search to find something—anything—that might prove of use in the litigation. This information also must not be privileged. Privileged information arises out of relationships granted qualified communication and testimonial immunity. Thus, information involving spouses, patient–doctor relations, or client–lawyer communications often is excluded from the discovery process. Most significant in this context is the client–lawyer relationship. The work product of an attorney generated in preparation for litigation—litigation strategies, memoranda, legal research and analysis, and drafts of briefs and legal papers—is explicitly excluded from the dictates of discovery. Last, although medical or mental examinations are permitted—and, in Jane's case, likely to be required—they generally require a court order based on their necessity to the case.

Concurrent with or immediately after the discovery process, many courts require active efforts by both parties to settle the case before trial. Generally, no one wants a trial. If a trial can be avoided on the basis of negotiation, it is generally in everyone's best interests to act accordingly. To this end, many state jurisdictions require mediation of the dispute by a neutral third party before a case can go to trial. Other states merely encourage voluntary mediation as a way for litigants to avoid the costs of litigation. At the federal level, mediation rules run the gamut from voluntary to mandatory on a district-by-district basis via court order. Pretrial mediation consists of retaining a neutral third-party advisor to assist the parties in a lawsuit in exploring settlement options: the mediator has no authority to impose outcomes. Mediators serve a facilitative role, using specialized communication and negotiation techniques as well as their experience in settling similar disputes, to assist the parties in discovering common ground on which to build a settlement. An alternative entails a pretrial conference with the judge in pursuit of the goal of ending the dispute to everyone's satisfaction or at least simplifying and streamlining the trial. Even the judge in a pretrial conference has limited authority to demand concessions from the parties. Should the mediation work, and it often does, the result is an out-of-court settlement and the end of the dispute. When it fails, the next step is to move on to the trial phase.

Before the trial, the parties in the case will have already selected the method by which the factual questions in dispute will be litigated. Legal questions are always the province of the judge. The judge determines what evidence can be presented, how the procedural rules shaping the litigation process will be implemented, and ultimately how the substantive laws associated with this dispute will be applied to the factual context of the dispute. Factual questions can also be decided by the judge, in a bench trial; or the litigants can elect to have a trial by jury in which a jury determines the specific factual elements necessary to determine the differences and disputes of the parties in a trial.

In our example, Jane or Dan elected to have a jury, and the judge determined it proper to hold a jury trial. The trial then formally begins with jury selection. Once the jury is chosen and seated, the formal proceedings begin with opening statements from the parties' lawyers designed to explain the broad outlines of the case to the jury, to introduce the jury to the parties' legal theories as to the proper outcome of the case, and finally to summarize the evidence to be presented in support of these theories. Traditionally, the plaintiff presents her opening statement first, because it is she who is making demands on the court for remedies. The defense then follows to explain how and why the plaintiff's contentions and theories are incorrect and the requested remedies are not called for. This pattern of argument by the plaintiff followed by the defendant continues throughout the trial.

With the opening statements completed, the trial moves on to the presentation of evidence in support of the contentions made in the opening statements. It is here, through the presentation of documents or physical artifacts and the questioning of witnesses, that the lawyers on both sides "make their case" to the jury. At all times, the evidence presented to the jury must be relevant to the dispute at hand, be based on direct knowledge and generally not on hearsay by the witness, not violate any privileged relationships, and, in the case of documents, be the original documents or reliable copies. Similarly, expert witnesses who can express opinions to the jury must first be certified by the court as an expert before giving their testimony. At any time, lawyers on the other side can challenge the information being provided as violating rules of evidence. It is then up to the judge to determine if the objection has merit. When it does, the judge will exclude such documents or testimony from the record where already given or deny the presentation of such documents or testimony if not yet in the formal court record. The judge also will instruct the jury to disregard such excluded matters.

Procedural rules also shape the way each side can present its evidence to the jury. When questioning witnesses whom they have called to the stand—what is known as direct examination— lawyers are limited to asking only open-ended questions (except when introducing the witness and for hostile witnesses—witnesses deemed supportive of the other side in the dispute). As with the logic behind discovery, the objective here is that the evidence persuades the jury, not the lawyer; open-ended questions place the witnesses and their knowledge front and center. Once the direct examination is completed, the lawyer for the other side is permitted to cross-examine the witness. Here, leading questions are permitted. Leading questions consist of questions in which the answer is implied or suggested in the question's wording. Thus, Jane's lawyer could ask Dan on cross examination, "Isn't it true that you regularly wet down your sidewalk? In fact, that you do this every morning and evening?" By asking leading questions, the lawyer can test and even undermine the credibility of the testimony the witness had given on direct examination—this is, in fact, the primary objective in cross-examination. On the completion of cross-examination, the originating lawyer is permitted to question the witness again (called redirect examination), subject to the same limits of direct examination, to attempt to re-establish the witness's credibility.

Once the plaintiff's attorney has concluded presenting all the evidence, both documentary and via witnesses, the defense attorney presents evidence. Before he or she begins, however, the defense attorney has the option of filing a special motion to dismiss. This motion argues that the plaintiff's presentation of the evidence failed to present adequate proof of the defendant's wrongdoing. With no reasonable case introduced against the defendant, there is no need for the trial to continue. If, after examining the plaintiff's case in the most favorable light for the plaintiff, the judge finds that no reasonable person would find in favor of the plaintiff, he may grant the motion, and the trial is over. Such motions are rarely granted, however. Whereas the strength of plaintiffs' cases can vary, it is rare that they do not present some facts supporting their contentions, enough to beat a dismissal motion; and in a trial by jury, judges like for the jury to hear both sides.

With that motion rejected, the trial continues with the defendant presenting documentary evidence and introducing and examining witnesses in support of his contentions and arguments. The same rules apply as during the plaintiff's presentation, but with the roles reversed. Thus, it is the defense who must use open-ended questions and the plaintiff who can ask leading questions on cross-examination. Upon completion of the defendant's case, both sides are permitted to make closing arguments in which they emphasize the testimony of their witnesses, point out the import of the documents they presented to the jury, and note the weaknesses and inconsistencies in the other side's evidence and arguments. With this, the trial phase is over.

Before the jury adjourns to render its verdict, the lawyers on both sides have the option of filing yet another motion, this one for a directed verdict. As with the defendant's motion to dismiss, the argument here is that the other side so failed in proving the factual basis of his or her case that no reasonable person could rule in that party's favor. This being so, there would be no reason for the jury to render a verdict; the judge could merely apply the law to the obvious factual elements of the case and render a final judgment. Here, too, the odds of success are small. In most cases, the judge will refuse the motion and send the jury out to deliberate.

Once sequestered, the jury members will organize themselves, pick a foreman, and then proceed to discuss and evaluate the evidence presented by both sides. Based on this evidence and guided in their deliberations by jury instructions issued by the judge and based on recommendations made by lawyers from each side (as to the scope and focus of the jury's efforts and the dictates of the law) and evaluating which side had the better case based on a preponderance of the evidence (typically explained as a 51 percent or more likelihood), the jury will render a verdict. Should the verdict be for the plaintiff, the jury will often then determine the proper amount of compensatory damages owed by the defendant necessary to return both parties to the position they would have been in had the defendant not caused harm to the plaintiff in the first place. In cases where punitive damages are appropriate, they would set this amount as well. Equitable remedies, should they be appropriate, remain the province of the judge. Should the jury rule in favor of the defendant, the jurors' job ends with the verdict.

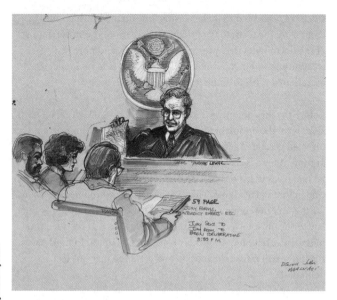

9. Federal district judge Pierre N. Leval instructs a jury on its duties as it sets out to decide a case.

For our example, Jane wins her case. The jury agrees that Dan's actions caused Jane to fall and hurt herself. Having calculated the monetary and nonmonetary losses to Jane, the jury determines that Dan owes Jane $50,000 in compensatory damages. As previously noted, given the facts of her case, no punitive damages are awarded or equitable remedies applied. With this decision in hand, the jury returns to the courtroom and their verdict and award are announced. The judge then issues his judgment based on the jury's findings and the jury is dismissed. The case, however, is not necessarily over.

Dan has available several posttrial motions. He can ask for a new trial based on the discovery of new evidence, questions as to the conduct of the jury in rendering its verdict, or errors in the production of evidence and the conduct of the trial. He could ask the judge for a judgment notwithstanding the verdict, arguing that no reasonable group of persons could have rendered the jury's verdict as a matter of law and asking the judge to therefore substitute his judgment in place of that of the jury. Or Dan can accept the jury's verdict but question the amount of the jury's award with a motion for relief from judgment.

Again, as with in-trial motions, the odds of Dan receiving a favorable result are usually small. They are not, however, nonexistent, and it costs Dan and his lawyer little to try. Yet, having failed in his attempts to overturn the jury's verdict or to minimize the mandated award, Dan's choices narrow to accepting the outcome and paying the award owed Jane or appealing the case to an intermediate appellate court. At this stage, the facts of the case are now largely frozen. Dan can no longer argue that it was Jane's fault that she got hurt. His appeal would have to involve some rather egregious mistake by the jury or error of law on the part of the trial judge. Perhaps the judge allowed some evidence that Dan and his lawyer believe should have been excluded. Or they think that the judge should have granted them a new trial or the judgment notwithstanding the verdict that they motioned for. On review, the appellate court would have the option of reversing the judgment of the trial court, remanding the case back to the trial court with instructions for further proceedings or rendering the judgment that it should have made, or affirming the judgment of the lower court. In this instance, the appellate judges affirm.

The case is now over. The dispute is ended—at least so long as Dan pays the court-ordered judgment. Should he fail to pay in a timely manner, Jane could return to the court seeking an order of execution directing a sheriff or court officer to seize funds and properties of Dan to be used to pay what he owes; in extreme cases of refusal to pay, Dan could face court-imposed penalties, the garnishment of wages, and even receivership, by which Dan's property would be administered and sold to cover the amount of the judgment.

Criminal cases

Though fundamentally different in purpose and result than civil cases, criminal cases share many of the same stages and procedures as a civil dispute. As with Jane's case, the defendant in a criminal matter will have to find a lawyer and discuss both the content of the case and the methods of payment (which will not include contingency fees as a payment option). There will be discovery and the rules shaping the testimony of witnesses will be the same. The order of the trial, the prosecution bringing the charges going first, followed by the defense, remains the same. Some of the motions and pleadings are also the same. And, of course, the role of the judge and jury remain unchanged (though the content of the jury's verdict will be different).

There are, however, many key differences between the two types of trials. Most fundamental are the consequences of losing. A lost civil dispute might cost one money or orders from a court demanding specific actions to remedy the dispute, but neither the defendant's life nor his or her liberty is at risk. In criminal cases they are. Possible punishments include fines and/or orders of restitution, lengthy probation periods, jail or prison time up to and including life in prison without parole, and, in the most extreme and increasingly rare cases, execution. The standards of proof necessary to convict are also different. Rather than a civil dispute's preponderance of the evidence (51 percent), criminal trials require proof of wrongdoing beyond a reasonable doubt. And the injured party is different. In civil cases, it is the victim of a wrong who brings the suit on their own behalf; in criminal matters the state stands as the aggrieved party—bringing suit against the defendant on behalf of the community in the name of public safety.

Another key difference is that, unlike a civil dispute, there is no transition period in which the courts are not involved. Courts are involved in criminal matters from the start. Even before charges are brought against the defendant, the judicial system is supervising the investigation and charging stages of the case. Among the rules they enforce are the protections provided the accused by the Bill of Rights, including the right against self-incrimination, protections from illegal search and seizure, the provision of a lawyer free of charge (if a defendant cannot afford one) at all significant stages of the criminal investigation, and the scheduling of a timely and public trial.

The interactions between the lawyers are also somewhat different. Unlike a civil case in which there is little pressure to settle other than wanting a suit to end quickly (and inexpensively), the negotiating power in a criminal matter lies mostly with the prosecution. They are the ones who have chosen the charges brought against the defendant, they have the full weight of the state backing their prosecutorial efforts, and they are motivated by more than a profit motive. Prosecutors take their jobs as the people's voice, as defenders of the public sphere, very seriously.

Still, negotiating and compromise remain key elements in a criminal trial. Crowded dockets, the need for speedy trials, and the necessities of seeing to the punishments of as many criminal defendants as possible foster a willingness on the part of prosecutors to negotiate plea bargains in which a defendant pleads guilty in return for a reduced sentence, a lowering of charges, or a mix of both. Defendants, for their part, generally welcome the chance to plea bargain. A negotiated plea deal not only means certainty as to the punishment assigned for the defendant's wrongful actions, but also usually a much less harsh set of punishments than would arise should the defendant plead not guilty and then lose at trial. Of course, pleading not guilty and winning means suffering no punishments; however, the odds of victory in a criminal case are rarely high enough to negate the advantages in certainty and leniency that a plea bargain brings. Put another way, the stakes in a criminal trial are generally greater than in a civil dispute—and higher stakes make for harder decisions. Ironically, this makes being truly innocent the worst thing one can be as a criminal defendant. The system is largely designed on the assumption that everyone brought before a criminal court is guilty of something, and thus the priorities are to mete appropriate punishments in as quick and appropriate a manner as possible.

Final thoughts

As with so much of this Very Short Introduction, this summary of criminal trials (and, to a lesser extent, civil trials) leaves out many details and exceptions that shape the individual elements of the scenarios and procedures just presented. Similarly, different jurisdictions will have different rules and procedures that could affect the steps and outcomes of a civil dispute or criminal case. Yet despite these limits and exceptions, these descriptions of the process of a legal dispute provide the broad outlines of what a litigant could expect to experience should they find themselves caught up in a court case, whether civil or criminal.

Chapter 6
Politics and policy

Courts do not operate in a vacuum. Though individually powerful, courts are but one piece of a network of institutions and agencies governing America. They constitute one-third of the primary branches of government—holding separate but equal authority with the legislative and executive branches. As part of that whole, courts inevitably interact with, and often struggle with, the other institutions that govern America. The outcomes of these struggles have consequences; despite ongoing efforts to insulate the courts from politics, they are inevitably affected by political, social, and economic trends—and conversely affect these realms by their rulings and decisions.

Constitutional foundations

When the founders wrote state constitutions between 1776 and 1781 and the federal Constitution in 1787, most imposed a distinct conceptual and practical separation of the three main functions of government: legislative, executive, and judicial. Legislatures wrote laws, executives enforced the laws, and the judiciary adjudicated the impact of these laws on the everyday needs of citizens. Their experiences with British government, in which Parliament amalgamated the legislative, executive, and judicial functions into a single institution, made clear to the authors of these documents that concentrated government was dangerous government. To

ensure that government power never became too centralized—
while still being adequate to meet the legitimate needs of society
for leadership and governmental services—the founders granted
powers to each separate branch to act, and then made sure that
none could effectively use these powers without the explicit
agreement (or, alternatively, the implicit acceptance) of each of
the other parts of government.

The method was simple in concept. Create three separated
branches of government with differing yet essential jobs. Grant
each branch powers within its realm of authority. Then give each
branch the ability, nay duty, to hinder the other two branches in
the implementation of these powers through the existence of
various overlapping responsibilities and functions. Only where the
three branches could agree on a single policy could the
government use its full measure of authority. Thus, on the federal
level, Congress was given the power to declare war, pass all laws
(though subject to a presidential veto), oversee the executive
branch, and authorize spending. The president had the job of
spending the money authorized by Congress, defending the nation
in times of war, appointing all federal officers (including judges),
and entering into treaties—with the "advice and consent of the
Senate"—while ensuring that all laws were faithfully executed.

The federal courts, meanwhile, had the job of applying the laws
passed by Congress (often as implemented by the president) and
thus settling the unique yet consequential conflicts that arose
under these laws between different people, between people and
the government, and between states and the federal government.
In addition, as articulated in 1803's *Marbury v. Madison*, the
Supreme Court claimed for the federal judiciary the authority to
determine the scope and content of the US Constitution, taking
on itself the power to invalidate laws or executive actions deemed
in conflict with the explicit contents and limits of the US
Constitution. (Not long after, state supreme courts took up this
interpretive mantel for their state constitutions.)

Generally denoted as *separation of powers* and *checks and balances*, this system of split but interconnected authority forms the framework of American government—operating not only on the federal level, but also in various permutations over time on the state level. It also all but ensures extensive policy conflicts among the three branches of government. To take one admittedly extreme example, consider the disagreements over congressional oversight, executive prerogatives, and differing conceptions as to the dictates of the rule of law that occurred in the third year of the Trump administration—each of which collectively spawned not only numerous court cases, but also the president's impeachment by the House of Representatives in 2019 and subsequent acquittal by the Senate in 2020. At its core, this conflict focused on vastly differing perceptions of the proper reach of executive power, with both the president and Congress claiming authority over the other branch. The judiciary, meanwhile, was brought into this conflict as each side turned to the courts to challenge specific policy initiatives by the other party—each seeking the court's endorsement of the constitutional accuracy of its policy choices— which demanded policy judgments by the courts based on their priorities. The result, at best, was constant and disruptive turmoil and, at worst, a government at war with itself, as each branch sought primacy at all costs for its constitutional vision and priorities.

Yet these sorts of policy differences among the three branches of government need not always be so acute and volatile; the future of American democracy need not be placed at risk every time as a result of this three-way tug-of-war. Tensions among the branches over everyday policy matters occur regularly. Every time the executive branch modifies the scope of a law passed by the legislature via administrative rules or executive orders, or legislatures refuse to fund an executive priority or pass a law challenging a president or governor's executive decision-making, or the fifty-one supreme courts rule on the scope and legitimacy of a statute, regulation, or executive order, a chance for conflict exists. And more often than not, this chance becomes reality. On matters large and small, fundamental or peripheral, the three branches of government stand in a state of dynamic tension forced to balance their own policy preferences with the conflicting perspectives of the other branches.

In most instances, these tensions are settled by negotiation and conciliation. Knowing the potential for policy conflicts to lead to chaos, the norm since the founding has been for each of the three branches to seek out a compromise acceptable to all parties wherever and whenever possible. Thus, the courts generally give significant deference to legislative and executive actions and legal interpretations in reviewing such laws and executive orders or regulations for constitutional adequacy, overturning each only where they perceive substantial violations of constitutional imperatives. Executives traditionally uphold and enforce laws passed by legislatures and judicial readings of constitutions even where they disagree with the underlying policy objectives, except, of course, when they feel such views threaten the well-being of the nation. And legislatures generally follow the executive's lead on many important policy topics (national defense or foreign policy at the national level, public safety and emergency relief at the state) or the lead of supreme courts on constitutional interpretation, unless those dictates counter the legislature's collective will as the people's representatives on such matters.

Of course, this process works only when each branch is willing to accept the policy views and preferences of the other branches as legitimate (though not necessarily ideal). And for most of our nation's history—and for most policy disputes—this has been the case. Whether through shared partisan affiliations, ideological perspectives, or simply a common goal of maintaining political order, the people who make up the three branches of American government routinely work together. The road to consensus may be contentious and the result to no one's particular liking, but ultimately, a balance is struck, an agreement is reached, and the full power of the government is used to meet the needs of the nation—except, that is, when this does not happen and we enter a period of constitutional crisis.

Judicial review and the US Supreme Court

For the courts, most policy disagreements with the other branches of government (federal or state) grow out of the judiciary's power of judicial review. In claiming the authority to define the scope and meaning of the Constitution, the US Supreme Court placed the federal courts in the center of a vortex in the debate over the proper scope, focus, and action of not only the federal government but also the state governments. When the court speaks with authority as to the meaning of the Constitution, this is supposed to end the discussion. (The same holds true for state courts of last resort on matters of state constitutional interpretation.) That noted, normally, the justices of the Supreme Court are reluctant to deploy these powers in an extreme, definitive manner. The underlying norm within courts of last resort is to find answers that bridge policy disagreements instead of exacerbating them. Yet, given the countless constitutional challenges argued before such courts, even a small number of exceptions in which the justices feel compelled to impose their preferred policy preferences (in the name of constitutional integrity) in opposition to those held by the legislative or executive branches can have a significant impact.

A full account of the long and rich history of the many intended and sometimes unintended policy impacts of rulings by courts of last resort (let alone courts at all levels) would fill volumes. What follows are illustrative examples and summaries of this process drawn from the history of the US Supreme Court. As products of the highest court in the nation, its rulings are some of the most politically consequential, and often controversial, within the entire American judicial system. We must keep in mind, however, that the US Supreme Court is not the only court to face these pressures to act or the only court to accede to them. Both state courts of last resort and intermediate appellate courts, state and federal, face the same challenges and have the same opportunities to shape government as the US Supreme Court. It is just that the Supreme Court, as the highest court of last resort in the nation with jurisdiction over all matters federal and constitutional arising from both state and lower federal courts, has the greatest scope for nation-changing consequences.

Examples of influential, and controversial, judicial policymaking by the Supreme Court started early. In 1793, the court held in *Chisholm v. Georgia* that states did not have sovereign immunity where such challenges were brought in federal courts by citizens of other states. By a 4–1 vote, the justices concluded that Article III, Section 2, of the Constitution—which empowered the federal courts to hear all cases "between a state and citizens of another state"—abrogated the states' sovereign immunity protections. This ruling proved so controversial that in less than a year Congress passed, and the states ratified, an Eleventh Amendment to the Constitution: "The judicial power of the United States shall not be construed to extend to any suit in law or equity, commenced or prosecuted against one of the United States by citizens of another state, or by citizens or subjects of any foreign state."

In 1810, the court found itself involved in another controversial, and politically explosive, matter. Following the end of the American Revolution, Georgia laid claim to all lands west of the state—known as the Yazoo lands—encompassing territory that later would become the states of Alabama and Mississippi. In 1795, the Georgia state legislature divided the Yazoo lands into four sections and sold the ownership rights to these sections to four separate land development companies for the (even then) admittedly very low price of $500,000 (about $0.014 per acre). Soon word got out that the Yazoo land's bargain prices had been the result of bribery in the state legislature. In the next election (1796), those legislators who had championed the sale were collectively voted out of office. The new legislature quickly repealed the law authorizing the Yazoo land sale, in the process voiding the title to these lands, not only of the land development companies that had bribed the original legislators, but also of anyone who had subsequently purchased the lands from these companies while the 1795 law was in effect.

Among those affected were Robert Fletcher and John Peck. Peck had speculated in the Yazoo lands in 1795, purchasing large tracts of land from the original development companies. Several years later, he sold portions of this land to Fletcher (despite the voiding of the original sale of the land by the Georgia legislature in 1796, Peck maintained his rights to the land he had purchased before this second law's enactment). Fletcher, wishing to ensure that his title to the land was legally protected, sued Peck in federal court in 1803, claiming fraud (for selling him land to which Peck did not have clear ownership). His hope, however, was to lose his case; the goal of the suit was to get the Supreme Court to rule the 1795 sale legal and the 1796 repeal illegal. This would ensure both Fletcher's and Peck's ownership rights to the land.

Under the leadership of chief justice John Marshall, the Supreme Court was more than willing to comply. Concerned about the negative economic effects of allowing state governments to void contracts unilaterally (even if the source of these contracts was questionable or even illegal), Marshall saw in *Fletcher v. Peck* the opportunity to protect private property from the whims of political change. Turning to the Constitution's contract clause, which forbade states from passing laws "impairing the Obligation of Contracts," the court unanimously ruled that the Georgia state legislature's repeal of the 1795 act was an unconstitutional act in violation of Article I, Section 10, of the US Constitution. Having once entered a contract, the state was legally bound to abide by the contract.

In this ruling, the court applied for the first time its power of judicial review to invalidate an unconstitutional state law—a power that the court would use regularly in the following decades as it sought to create a uniform commercial environment despite the extensive conflicts between differing state laws. In such cases as *McCulloch v. Maryland* (1819), *Dartmouth College v. Woodward* (1819), *Cohens v. Virginia* (1821), *Gibbons v. Ogden* (1824), *Charles River Bridge v. Warren Bridge* (1837), *Swift v. Tyson* (1842), and *Ableman v. Booth* (1859), the court ruled in various ways to stress the power of the national government in general, and the federal courts in particular, to impose economic and procedural rules applicable to all states.

Even when the court changed its stance on the best methods to protect property rights (shifting from a hard stance in defense of existing property rights to a more flexible stance that allowed for the "creative destruction" of old property by newer methods of producing wealth), the goal of creating a safe national marketplace in which Americans from all states could do business remained in place through the Civil War and the reminder of the nineteenth century.

Sometimes the court's willingness to impose its own policy preferences arose in response to times of legal, constitutional, and political crisis. In the 1850s, the United States was literally tearing itself apart over the incompatibilities inherent in a nation divided by slaveholding and nonslaveholding regions. These tensions were most notable as regarded the issue of how to organize the common territories for settlement—in particular, whether to allow slavery to establish itself in these territories. The North largely wanted to exclude slavery from the territories; the South wanted to permit its expansion.

Throughout the first decades of the nineteenth century, several legislative compromises had sought to constrain this competition for land. In 1820, in the Missouri Compromise, Congress agreed to split the lands that the nation had acquired in 1803 by the Louisiana Purchase along a north/south divide. Taking the southern border of Missouri (which became a slave state with Maine coming in as a free state) as its dividing line, the compromise permitted slavery only south of this line. In the North, slavery would be prohibited. In 1850, facing the dilemma of incorporating the lands acquired from Mexico as a result of the Mexican–American War, Congress passed a complicated mix of laws (soon called the Compromise of 1850) that brought California into the Union as a free state while ending the slave trade in Washington, DC, and simultaneously imposing a much stronger, federally enforced fugitive slave law long desired by Southerners. The remaining lands seized from Mexico were split between free territories (Utah and Nevada) and territories in which the choice of slavery or freedom would be put off to a later date for determination by the people of the territory (New Mexico and Arizona), a doctrine known as popular sovereignty. Finally, in 1854, to appease pro-slavery Southerners who objected to most of the Louisiana Purchase lands being identified as free territories, Congress passed the Kansas–Nebraska Act, repealing the Missouri Compromise and making the status of slavery in all remaining lands in the Louisiana Purchase subject to a decision on the slave question by those living in these territories.

The Kansas–Nebraska Act proved highly disruptive. Soon political parties fragmented (the Whigs), new parties formed (the Republicans), and tensions between the North and the South grew ever more explosive, with outright violence both within the territories (Bleeding Kansas) and in Congress itself (the caning of Massachusetts senator Charles Sumner by South Carolina congressman Preston Brooks) the result. This is where the Supreme Court stepped in. In 1857 the court had before it a freedom suit by a Missouri slave, Dred Scott, who argued that his time living with his master in the then-free territory of Minnesota had dissolved his slave status. Having once lived in a free territory, Scott argued, he was now a free man.

Though Southern state courts had upheld lawsuits of this sort in the early years of the nineteenth century, by the 1850s, they no longer were willing to accept such arguments as valid. Once a slave, always a slave; put another way—slavery national, freedom local. The question was whether the US Supreme Court would support the older doctrinal precedents (which viewed slavery as local and freedom as national) or agree with the South's newer reading on the universality and permanence of slavery. In the end, the court sided with the South—sort of. The court's response to Dred Scott's petition for freedom was highly fragmented. Each of the nine justices issued his own separate opinion on the case; none of the opinions agreed completely on the specifics of the case or its legal resolution. Still, only two justices argued that Scott should be a free man; the remaining seven justices held Scott to still be a slave. However, none of the seven justices in the majority could agree on the specifics as to why Scott should remain a slave. Into this conceptual breach strode chief justice Roger B. Taney.

Taney, from slaveholding southern Maryland, was deeply troubled by the state of politics in America. He saw the nation pulling itself apart on the issue of slavery, and he believed that it was the job of his court to provide a definitive constitutional answer to the dilemmas posed by slavery and the presence of millions of African Americans on American soil. Since the court collectively could not provide this definitive solution, he would take it on himself to do so. Using his administrative power as chief justice, Taney made sure that when the opinions of the court in *Dred Scott v. Sandford* were published, his opinion went first. Traditionally, the first opinion listed is the "opinion of the court." All that follow are concurrences or dissents. Hence, normally, it is the first opinion from whence precedent flows and the Constitution's full meaning is found. Such was not the case here. No other justices had joined Taney's opinion. Though seven of them agreed as to the result— Scott was still a slave—none agreed with Taney's reading as to the why or how of this result, or with Taney's ultimate conclusions as to the Constitution's dictates. Consequently, Taney's opinion had no more precedential value than any of the other eight. Yet none of this stopped Taney; ignoring the technicalities as to sources of precedent and as to the Constitution's dictates, Taney acted as if his opinion was the court's opinion of record.

What was Taney's answer to the dilemma of slavery in America? He placed slavery under the Constitution's protection. Declaring the already repealed 1820 Missouri Compromise unconstitutional (and, incidentally, the popular sovereignty solution of the 1854 Kansas–Nebraska Act), Taney argued that the common territories had to be accessible to all Americans equally. That accessibility, in turn, had to include federal protection of the property of those Americans entering the common territories—including a Southerner's property in his slaves. By explicitly excluding slave property from the northern half of the Louisiana Purchase, Congress had both discriminated against Southerners and failed to abide by the Fifth Amendment's prohibition of expropriation of private property by government without due process and just compensation, Taney argued. Viewed properly, he maintained, the Fifth Amendment demanded that the federal government actively protect the property of slaveholders in the common territories.

Unwilling to stop here, Taney next held that African Americans were not, nor could ever be, citizens of the United States. African Americans—slave or free—were an inferior race whose rights and privileges within the United States were essentially the gift of the white race. As noncitizens of the United States, it was up to each individual state to determine how to treat its African American population—and the federal government's role to accept these state decisions as authoritative. Hence, if Missouri considered Dred Scott a slave, he was a slave; his sojourn in an improperly designated "free territory" was irrelevant to the matter of Scott's status. Finally, Taney insisted that in promulgating this solution, he was only following the original intentions of the framers of the Constitution. Problem solved—or so Taney concluded.

Of course, Taney's "solution" to the slavery problem solved nothing. In fact, it made matters worse, because the South thereafter demanded federal protection of their slave property in the common territories (and on the eve of the Civil War, in the free states as well), whereas the North adamantly disagreed with Taney's assessment of the Constitution and the race question, using it as "proof" of the South's designs to make America into a "slave nation." Ultimately, it would take a Civil War, three civil rights amendments to the US Constitution, and almost a century of Supreme Court rulings and congressional enactments even to work out partly the dilemma of race and rights in America at the heart of *Dred Scott*. Not surprisingly, given the events that followed, Taney's attempt to solve on his own the race issue in America went down as perhaps the worst decision of the US Supreme Court.

Second on many people's list of terrible Supreme Court rulings was 1905's *Lochner v. New York*. This case set forth the high court's decision to solve "definitively" a nagging political, constitutional, and economic quandary: the question of defining the proper scope (and limits) of government to regulate the use and accumulation of private property.

In the years following the end of the Civil War, as America's economy rapidly expanded, in part because of the rise of large interstate corporations, a growing divide arose between those with property and those without. Farmers, labor, and small businessmen all complained about the "abuses" of the ever-growing industrial and transportation corporations. They felt trapped in an economy and political system that empowered those who already had property to gain more, while hindering the ability of those who labored ever to get ahead. Recognizing the power that raw numbers provided in a democracy, these laboring classes turned to state government, demanding the regulation of economic abuses by large interstate corporations. The result, starting in the 1870s, was a series of ever more specific laws regulating the business practices of interstate corporations, matched with the creation of regulatory agencies whose task was the enforcement of these regulatory laws. In the 1880s and 1890s, the federal government joined in, with the creation of the Interstate Commerce Commission (1887) to supervise common carriers (railroads and later trucking companies) and the enactment of the Sherman Anti-Trust Act (1890), empowering the government to break up large corporations acting "in restraint of trade."

Worried about the potential of unfettered government regulations to expropriate what they saw as "honestly" earned wealth to the benefit of the voting (but largely propertyless) masses, the US Supreme Court applied the Fourteenth Amendment (which held that "nor shall any State deprive any person of life, liberty, or property, without due process of law") to protect corporate property from "excessive" governmental interference by legislative enactment or executive regulatory agencies. Most notable in this regard were a series of cases in which the Supreme Court held that regulations limiting the rates that railroads could charge had to be "reasonable" in their impact—a subjective standard that effectively left federal judges free to impose their own standards of reasonable in place of that arrived at by administrative agencies or even state legislatures.

Court opposition to business regulations did not stop the demands for reform. By the turn of the twentieth century, with the rise of the Progressive movement, both the state and the federal governments were increasing their efforts to regulate what they saw as the abuses of corporate power damaging the well-being of the American people. One such effort was New York's 1895 Bakeshop Act. Passed as a public health measure, the act limited the hours that bakers could work in a week. The legislature's fear was that excessive labor in badly ventilated bakeries could sicken bakers, who would then transmit their illness to those buying the bread they baked.

Joseph Lochner, a small-time baker in Utica, New York, argued that the law was unconstitutional. The Fourteenth Amendment's due process protections, Lochner argued, gave him and his workers the unfettered right to negotiate a contract to secure the best interests of both parties. Barring clear evidence of a significant public health threat—a condition that Lochner argued did not exist in most bakeries—the state had no right to impose its judgment as to the proper working hours of bakers for those who did the work. The New York courts disagreed. The Bakeshop Act, they held, was a legal use of the state's police powers to protect the safety of the state's inhabitants.

In 1905, the US Supreme Court took the case on appeal. Though it had recently upheld a Utah law regulating the hours that miners could work (in 1898's *Holden v. Hardy*), in a 5–4 decision the court invalidated the New York Bakeshop Act as an impermissible violation of the "liberty to contract" enjoyed by workers. Barring a clear public health or safety violation (which the majority did not see in this case, despite the state legislature's investigation and documentation of such facts), New York had no right to interpose its standards to replace the information guiding those engaged in labor contract negotiations. To do so would be to deprive independent workers of their constitutional rights as free individuals to seek to control the conditions of their labor via contract negotiations. That most laborers had unequal bargaining leverage in these negotiations was irrelevant. If workers did not like the outcome of their negotiations, they could seek other work.

The *Lochner* ruling was not without controversy. There is a good reason many consider it one of the court's worst opinions. Once again, the justices were imposing their policy judgments as to the legitimacy of a state regulation (i.e., the public safety implications of the Bakeshop Act) over the informed judgment of the executive or legislative branches. In this case, the majority did so largely in support of an economic theory (liberty of contract) not found in the Constitution's text. As justice Oliver Wendell Holmes Jr. noted in dissent, the majority's ruling was "decided upon an economic theory which a large part of the country does not entertain." Emphasizing that "a constitution is not intended to embody a particular economic theory," Holmes concluded by noting that the "Fourteenth Amendment does not enact Mr. Herbert Spencer's *Social Statics*" (a book advocating strict *laissez faire*, or "hands-off," philosophy of government economic regulations).

In subsequent years, the court continued to impose its views on economic matters over that of executive and legislative pronouncements as regarded "yellow-dog contracts" (*Coppage v. Kansas*), federal anti–child labor laws (*Hammer v. Dagenhart*), and minimum-wage laws (*Adkins v. Children's Hospital*). In 1935 and 1936, the Supreme Court invalidated almost all the measures constituting the entire early New Deal adopted by Congress to combat the Great Depression. In fact, only after a series of rulings in 1937 upholding the late New Deal (brought on partly by evolving constitutional views by some justices and later by a shift in the court's personnel) would the justices agree to stop imposing their policy preferences instead of following the policy choices of the legislature or executive on economic matters.

Civil rights and liberties in the Supreme Court

The court's abandonment of intervening in economic policymaking in the decades after 1937 did not portend that the court was forsaking policy debates with the other branches of government. The court was still ready to engage in policy debates when the justices felt that the Constitution required action. What changed was the focus of the court's concerns: now they were more about individual rights and liberties, not only property rights. The result, if anything, expanded the scope of the court's reach and the number of court rulings demanding specific policy results at odds with other elements of the government.

The targets here were state (and some federal) laws that denied due process and equal protection of the laws to the disadvantaged of society. Denials of due process and the unequal application of law to people of different races, ethnicities, and genders were rampant across the nation. Despite the protections guaranteed by the Bill of Rights and the Fourteenth Amendment, little had been done to apply these constitutional provisions to prevent such legal injuries to rights and equality. Much of the blame lay with the Supreme Court itself. Facing an expansive Bill of Rights, three civil rights amendments, and multiple civil rights and enforcements acts all aimed at ending disparate treatment under the law for the disadvantaged, the justices balked.

In 1833's *Barron v. Mayor & City Council of Baltimore*, the court abandoned all pretense of protecting the civil liberties promised by the Bill of Rights. Ruling that, as the first ten "amendments [to the US Constitution] contain no expression indicating an intention to apply them to the State governments," the justices decreed that "this court cannot so apply them." Put another way, unless a specific constitutional provision explicitly addressed the states, the US Constitution restrained only the federal government. As for the federal government, the justices found few occasions throughout the nineteenth and early twentieth centuries in which federal laws crossed the line into outright violations of the Bill of Rights.

Meanwhile, in a series of rulings in the second half of the nineteenth century, the court undermined the reach of the civil rights amendments. In the *Slaughterhouse Cases* (1873), they limited the "privileges and immunities" of citizenship to only those granted by the federal government—and defined these federal protections in the narrowest of terms. In the *Civil Rights Cases* (1883), the court held that the due process and equal protection provisions of the Fourteenth Amendment covered only public acts by state government officials; private discrimination was not prohibited under the law. In *Mills v. Green* (1895) and *Giles v.*

Harris (1903), the court upheld the near-total disenfranchisement of African American men despite the clear wording of the Fifteenth Amendment protecting their right to vote. And, in *Plessy v. Ferguson* (1896), the justices accepted the legal fiction of "separate but equal" as permitting the legal separation of the races that lay at the heart of Jim Crow segregation.

By the middle decades of the twentieth century, the court had reversed course on rights and equality. Taking a piecemeal approach, the court began slowly to incorporate individual elements of the Bill of Rights to bind the states on a case-by-case basis. Beginning with freedom of speech and of the press, the court soon moved on to freedom of religion and most notably to the rights of the accused to due process. Contemporaneously, the court tackled the contentious and controversial problem of equal protection of the laws based on race, ethnicity, and later gender, ending discrimination in its many forms—from segregated schools to disenfranchisement, housing restrictions to a woman's right to control her own reproductive processes.

In almost all these instances, the court took on existing laws and procedures and, proceeding case by case, declared them invalid. No longer could the government ignore religious convictions of those who came under the nation's laws (at least as long as those convictions did not produce acts illegal under other constitutional laws). Limits on freedom of speech, assembly, and an individual's right to own a gun for self-defense were declared in most instances unconstitutional. Those accused of a crime gained a profusion of new constitutional protections and publicly funded services, each aimed at correcting existing legal rules that unfairly (and unconstitutionally) stacked the deck against defendants. And, though it took some time to get the court started in a consistent manner, it also declared invalid discriminatory racial, ethnic, and, to a lesser extent, gender laws and imposed remedial efforts to repair the damage.

The results rocked the nation to its foundations. Few of these new constitutional interpretations were popular at the time of their adoption. Legislators and executives from both the national and the state governments repeatedly cried foul. Many legislators proposed constitutional amendments reversing these rulings (only to fail to get them through Congress). The justices were attacked personally and collectively; some members of the Supreme Court faced serious calls for impeachment. Pledges of massive resistance and demagogues' encouragement of violent reactions by angry mobs caused political and social turmoil across the nation. The discovery by the court of an implied right to privacy—directed primarily toward issues of reproductive rights and marriage equality—set off generations of constitutional battles over abortion, gay rights, and women's rights; these controversies still rage in the early twenty-first century.

In the end, as with most controversial struggles between the branches of government (or between the federal and state governments), compromises were worked out. In some instances, what were initially seen as entirely unacceptable overreach by the court came to be viewed as manageable disagreements whose details could be modified in subsequent litigations or with the passage of remedial legislation acceptable to all (such as shifting views on the actual usefulness of the *Miranda* warnings given by police officers outlining the accused's constitutional rights). In other instances, the legislative and executive branches came to see the value in the court's demands for change, implementing legislation and policies that took matters far beyond the court's initial forays into these matters. In still others, the legislative and executive branches came to accept the court's dictates as to the proper reach and scope of the Constitution, adapting in time to the changes demanded (though with regular complaints as to the need to adapt). Only a handful of matters, such as those noted previously or reforms such as affirmative action, remained open wounds—continually fought over as new cases were brought before the court challenging the status quo again and again.

Yet for all its controversy and seeming distinctiveness, this whirlwind of judicial action was not a new phenomenon. The Supreme Court has always been an activist body, interposing its policy preferences in place of those of the state governments or Congress and the president. What was different was the focus of this activism. For 150 years, the court's primary policy concerns were economic nationalism and property; now they were individual rights and liberties. This change in focus made the court's actions appear more aggressive, more demanding, more controversial, and more impactful. And, as with these earlier periods of judicial activism, this extended period of judicial imposition of court preferences on policymaking brought about a backlash.

Doctrinal and practical opposition to the court's civil rights and civil liberties rulings never fully went away. Whereas overall the legislative, executive, and judicial players in this process seemed to find a satisfactory middle ground of policy actions, legislative workarounds, and legal principles that incorporated the court's reading of the Constitution, a counterattack was building. Starting with Richard Nixon, Republican presidents, governors, and legislators ran political campaigns actively attacking the "activist" liberal judges of the Supreme Court. Conservative legal academics, pundits, and theoreticians constructed alternative legal and policy agendas and pushed different readings of constitutional imperatives. Slowly, conservative justices who opposed the "liberal excesses" of the court's civil rights and civil liberties pronouncements joined the court. By the late 1980s and 1990s, these conservative justices balanced the court's liberal justices. The momentum of pro–civil rights and civil liberties rulings slowed drastically, and new decisions from the court began to chip away at some of the precedents these earlier cases had set.

With the start of a new millennium, the balance finally tipped. Though gay rights and marriage equality were written into the equal protection clause in *Lawrence v. Texas* (2003) and *Obergefell v. Hodges* (2015), overall, the past twenty years have seen a concerted assault by the court on such civil rights and civil liberties.

To take one example of the court's turn to conservative readings of the Constitution, consider the linked topics of voting rights enforcement and partisan gerrymanders (the intentional effort to manipulate a legislative boundary to favor one party over the other). The passage in 1965 of a Voting Rights Act gave the federal government the duty to protect the rights of minorities to a fair and equal vote. Following the 2010 Census, legislators in mostly Republican-controlled states began to draw new districts to minimize aggressively the electoral success of the opposition party. Their method was simple: either they packed as many Democrats into a single district as possible (making the surrounding districts majority Republican) or they cracked apart democratic majorities into multiple districts in which the Democrats made up a minority of the voters. In either case, the result was the creation of "safe" districts, almost guaranteeing victory for the party drawing the new districts.

These outcomes did not go unnoticed or unchallenged. Voters, civil rights groups, and political parties brought suits in state and federal courts contesting the partisan nature of newly drawn districts. In most instances, the plaintiffs won their suits at the trial court level. Some even succeeded at the next level of federal appellate courts. In the state courts, plaintiffs won before the highest courts in the state. But not before the US Supreme Court.

In June 2019, the US Supreme Court held in *Rucho v. Common Cause* that federal courts were powerless to hear challenges to partisan gerrymandering laws. Legislative redistricting, Chief

10. The power of judicial review often results in conflict between the US Supreme Court and the executive or legislative branches. A 1974 cartoon by Pat Oliphant, in which the justices wear football helmets and the scoreboard reads "Supreme Court 8, White House 0," depicts this tension in *United States v. Nixon*.

Justice Roberts noted for a 5–4 majority, was an inherently political task, one explicitly given by the Constitution to the state legislatures to complete. The federal courts, in turn, were limited by the Constitution to deciding only legal questions. As such, "we conclude that partisan gerrymandering claims present political questions beyond the reach of the federal courts"—even though lower federal courts and state courts were finding innovative and effective ways to manage the complexities of partisan gerrymandering.

The courts as political actors

In the end, it should come as little surprise that the US Supreme Court has been, and continues to be, a highly political institution whose rulings not only have significant political impact but also are often shaped out of the policy preferences of the sitting justices. Courts of last resort are policymaking bodies. It may be legal or constitutional policies they are shaping, but in the end, all policy is political. Consequently, policy differences and efforts to impose their policy preferences over that of the other branches of government are simply a function of the American system of separation of powers and checks and balances.

And as with courts of last resort (state or federal), the same forces shape the output of most intermediate appellate courts. Given the small number of cases courts of last resort generally hear in a year, intermediate appellate courts provide the vast majority of rulings having lasting policymaking effects. The raw numbers are simply on their side. Even trial courts have this impact when the matter before them raises new or controversial topics.

The point, once again, is that such controversy and contention between the branches of government is not an exception to the rules and procedures shaping government policymaking—they are the inevitable outcome of these rules and procedures. Once one moves beyond the personal impacts a court ruling can have on litigants, this is where the American judicial system can—and does—have its greatest impacts.

Afterword

This book began by noting the tensions lurking within the term *the American judicial system*. On a structural level, the United States does not have one judicial system, but fifty-one. Each state and the federal government have a unique take on the necessities and structures of providing judicial services to those they serve. Yet in the end, the services demanded and the general approaches to providing these services merge into a messy whole.

We do have *an American judicial system*, which fulfills an essential role in maintaining the well-being of the nation. True, other institutions could fill these roles and provide these services. But in America the courts have been tasked with settling disputes, upholding rules and norms, providing authoritative oversight to changing social and economic relationships, sanctioning wrongdoing, and shaping public policies across a wide range of topics.

From the lowest courts of limited jurisdiction to the highest court in the land, judicial institutions provide essential services that keep the United States running. The roles they serve and the functions they provide may be different, but each is necessary, even essential. Without judges and lawyers and jurors, all doing their jobs; without state and federal courts providing both local and national remedies to legal and practical dilemmas; without the review process that appellate courts use to ensure uniformity of the law; without these and so many other roles and functions spread out across the whole of the judicial pyramid, there would be less order, less safety, less justice in this country. We depend on courts for so much. Overworked as they so often are, hampered by the diversity that a federal system of laws produces, they meet our needs.

References

Preface: The contours of the American judicial system

The total count of American judicial systems is technically fifty-two—
    if we include the municipal courts of Washington, DC—or even up
    to fifty-four if we include the military judicial system and Native
    American judicial systems as separate court systems—however,
    this Very Short Introduction does not include these judicial
    systems for simplicity's sake.

Chapter 1: Structures and jurisdictions

On John Adams's statement that ours is "a government of laws, and
    not of men": "Massachusetts Constitution, 2nd March, 1780," in
    The Founders Constitution, ed. Philip B. Kurland and Ralph
    Lerner (Indianapolis, IN: Liberty Fund, 2000): 1:14. Also available
    online at http://press-pubs.uchicago.edu/founders/print_
    documents/v1ch1s6.html.

On caseload comparisons, see R. LaFountain, S. Strickland,
    R. Schauffler, K. Holt, and K. Lewis, *Examining the Work of State
    Courts: An Overview of 2013 State Court Caseloads* (Williamsburg,
    VA: National Center for State Courts, 2015), 6; "State Court
    Caseload Digest, 2017," National Center for State Courts, https://
    www.courtstatistics.org/__data/assets/pdf_file/0021/29820/2017-
    Digest-print-view.pdf; "Federal Judicial Caseload Statistics: 2017,"
    United States Courts, https://www.uscourts.gov/judicial-caseload-
    indicators-federal-judicial-caseload-statistics-2017; "Federal
    Judicial Caseload Statistics: 2019," United States Courts, Table C-4,

https://www.uscourts.gov/report-names/federal-judicial-caseload-statistics; *Colorado Judicial Branch Annual Statistical Report: Fiscal Year 2014*, Colorado Courts, Tables 13 and 14, https://www.courts.state.co.us/userfiles/file/Administration/Planning_and_Analysis/Annual_Statistical_Reports/2014/Annual%20Statistical%20Report%20FY2014%20FINAL.pdf; *Annual Statistical Report for the Texas Judiciary—2015*, State of Texas Judicial Branch, http://www.txcourts.gov/media/1308021/2015-ar-statistical-print.pdf; Paula Hannaford-Agor, Scott Graves, and Shelley Spacek Miller, *Civil Justice Initiative: The Landscape of Civil Litigation in State Courts* (Williamsburg, VA: National Center for State Courts, 2015), 31, https://www.ncsc.org/~/media/Files/PDF/Research/CivilJusticeReport-2015.ashx.

The quote on jurisdiction comes from International Shoe Co. v. Washington, 326 U.S. 310, 316 (1945).

Chapter 2: Roles and functions

On precedent cases, see Hopwood v. Texas, 78 F.3d 932 (5th Cir. 1996); Regents of the University of California v. Bakke, 438 U.S. 265 (1978); Grutter v. Bollinger, 539 U.S. 306 (2003); United States v. Collazo, No. 15–05009 (9th Cir. Dec. 2, 2020).

Chief justice John Marshall's statement that the job of the US Supreme Court is to "say what the law is" comes from Marbury v. Madison, 5 U.S. (1 Cranch) 137, 178.

On caseloads in courts of last resort: "The Justices' Caseloads," Supreme Court of the United States, https://www.supremecourt.gov/about/courtatwork.aspx; "Federal Judicial Caseloads, 1789–2016," Federal Judicial Center, https://www.fjc.gov/history/exhibits/graphs-and-maps/supreme-court-caseloads-1880-2015; Matthew E. K. Hall and Jason Harold Windett, "New Data on State Supreme Court Cases," *State Politics & Policy Quarterly* 13 (December 2013): 436.

Quote by justice Sandra Day O'Connor: *This Honorable Court: Part 2, Inside the Marble Temple* (Washington, DC: York Zimmeran, 1988).

Quote by Alexander Hamilton: *Federalist*, no. 78, http://avalon.law.yale.edu/18th_century/fed78.asp.

On "repeat players" and "one-shotters," see Marc Galanter, "Why the 'Haves' Come Out Ahead: Speculations on the Limits of Legal Change," *Law and Society Review* 9, no. 1 (1974): 165–230.

On cases of first impression, see Monell v. Department of Soc. Svcs., 436 U.S. 658 (1978); Raynor v. State of Maryland, No. 1629 (Sep. 29, 2011).

Chapter 4: People

The quote from justice Oliver Wendell Holmes comes from Oliver Wendell Holmes Jr., *The Common Law* (Cambridge, MA: Belknap Press, 2009), 1.

"Report: Guilty Pleas on the Rise, Criminal Trials on the Decline," *The Innocence Project*, August 7, 2018, https://www.innocenceproject.org/guilty-pleas-on-the-rise-criminal-trials-on-the-decline/.

"2016–2018 Statistics," *American Bar Association*, https://www.americanbar.org/groups/legal_education/resources/statistics/; "New ABA Data Reveals Raise in Number of U.S. Lawyers, 15 Percent Increase since 2008," American Bar Association, May 11, 2018, https://www.americanbar.org/news/abanews/aba-news-archives/2018/05/new_aba_data_reveals/; "Number of Law Graduates in the U.S., 2013–2019," https://statista.com/statistics/428985/number-of-law-graduates-us; Joseph Sanders, "Courts and Law in Japan," in *Courts, Law, and Politics in Comparative Perspective*, ed. Herbert Jacob, Erhard Blankenburg, Herbert M. Kritzer, Doris Marie Provine, and Joseph Sanders (New Haven, CT: Yale University Press, 1996), 320.

Chapter 6: Politics and policy

Cases and constitutional sections on Supreme Court and economic nationalism: Marbury v. Madison, 5 U.S. 137 (1803); Chisholm v. Georgia, 2 U.S. 419 (1793); Amendment XI of the U.S. Constitution; Fletcher v. Peck, 10 U.S. 87 (1810); Article I, Section 10, Clause 1, of the U.S. Constitution; McCulloch v. Maryland, 17 U.S. 204 (1819); Dartmouth College v. Woodward, 17 U.S. 518 (1819); Cohens v. Virginia, 19 U.S. 264 (1821); Gibbons v. Ogden, 22 U.S. 1 (1824); Charles River Bridge v. Warren Bridge, 36 U.S. 420 (1837); Swift v. Tyson, 41 U.S. 1 (1842); Ableman v. Booth, 62 U.S. 506 (1859).

On changing views toward property protections and the doctrine of "creative destruction," compare the court's rulings in Dartmouth College v. Woodward, 17 U.S. (4 Wheat.) 518 (1819) to Charles River Bridge v. Warren Bridge, 36 U.S. (11 Pet.) 420 (1837).

Supreme Court and slavery: Dred Scott v. Sandford, 60
U. S. 393 (1857).

Supreme Court and economic regulation: Wabash, St. Louis, and
Pacific Railway Co. v. Illinois (the Wabash Case), 118 U.S. 557
(1886); Chicago, Milwaukee and St. Paul RR v. Minnesota (the
Minnesota Rate Cases), 134 U.S. 418 (1890); Reagan v. Farmers'
Loan and Trust Co., 154 U.S. 362 (1894); ICC v. Cincinnati, New
Orleans & Texas Pacific Railway Co., 167 U.S. 479 (1897); Smyth v.
Ames, 171 U.S. 361 (1898); Lochner v. New York, 198 U.S. 45
(1905); Coppage v. Kansas, 236 U.S. 1 (1995); Hammer v.
Dagenhart, 247 U.S. 251 (1918); Adkins v. Children's Hospital, 261
U.S. 525 (1923); A. L. A. Schechter Poultry Corp v. U. S., 295 U.S. 495
(1935); Louisville Joint Stock Land Bank v. Radford, 295 U.S. 555
(1935); U.S. v. Butler, 297 U.S. 1 (1936); Carter v. Carter Coal Co.,
298 U.S. 238 (1936); NLRB v. Jones & Laughlin Steel Corp., 301
U.S. 1 (1937); Steward Machine Co. v. Davis, 301 U.S. 548 (1937);
U.S. v. Darby Lumber Co., 312 U.S. 100 (1941); Wickard v. Filburn,
317 U.S. 111 (1942).

On the Supreme Court and civil liberties and civil rights: Barron v.
Mayor & City Council of Baltimore, 32 U.S. 243 at 250 (1833); The
Slaughterhouse Cases, 83 U.S. 36 (1873); The Civil Rights Cases,
109 U.S. 3 (1883); Mills v. Green, 159 U.S. 651 (1895); Giles v.
Harris, 189 U.S. 475 (1903); Plessy v. Ferguson, 163 U.S. 537
(1896); Everson v. Board of Education, 330 U.S. 1 (1947); Gitlow v.
New York, 268 U.S. 652 (1925); Mapp v. Ohio, 367 U.S. 643 (1961);
Ker v. California, 374 U.S. 23 (1963); Malloy v. Hogan, 378 U.S. 1
(1964); Klopfer v. North Carolina, 386 U.S. 213 (1967); Gideon v.
Wainwright, 372 U.S. 335 (1963); Lawrence v. Texas, 539 U.S. 558
(2003); Obergefell v. Hodges, 576 U.S. 644 (2015).

On the Supreme Court and gerrymandering: Rucho v. Common
Cause, 588 U.S. ___ (2019).

Further reading

A wide number of books and online resources explore the workings of the American judicial system. Most are much longer and go into much more detail than this Very Short Introduction. What follows is a very short introduction to readings in the many topics that describe the workings of the American judicial system.

For those looking for comprehensive books about America's courts and judicial processes, textbooks are the only real place to turn. To the good, most of these textbooks are well written and very comprehensive; to the negative, they are textbooks and hence can be a bit dry. Still, for those wishing more, some good starting points are Robert A. Carp et al., *The Judicial Process in America*, 11th ed. (Washington, DC: CQ Press, 2019); Lawrence Baum, *American Courts: Process and Policy*, 7th ed. (Boston: Cengage Learning, 2012); Frank August Schubert, *Introduction to Law and the Legal System*, 11th ed. (Boston: Cengage Learning, 2014); Michael L. Luenger and Paul J. De Muniz, *American Judicial Power: The State Court Perspective* (Northampton, MA: Edward Elgar, 2016); and Pamela C. Corley, Artemus Ward, and Wendy L. Martinek, *American Judicial Process: Myth and Reality in Law and Courts* (New York: Routledge, 2015).

In addition to textbooks, a wide array of articles explore the judicial process. Many have been collected into readers that provide a good summation of the scholarly literature on the topic of courts. The best and most informative is Elliot E. Slotnick, ed., *Judicial Politics: Readings from* Judicature, 2nd ed. (Washington, DC: CQ Press, 2005). *Judicature*, which sadly no longer publishes, was a journal aimed at judges. In it, legal and political science scholars presented their current research in a manner accessible to nonexperts (read: minimizing the math and statistics). Slotnick pulls some of the best of these essays together in a convenient single volume.

Another interesting and useful compendium of articles is presented by David M. O'Brien in *Judges on Judging: Views from the Bench*, 1st–5th eds. (Washington, DC: CQ Press, 1997–2016). As the title suggests, these books include a wide range of articles published by judges on the art and science of judging. While some seminal articles are included in each volume, each new edition removes some of the existing articles and adds new articles expanding on the scope of judges' reflections on their jobs. Taken together, these books are an amazing examination of the role, powers, and limitations of judges.

Other useful compendiums of articles on the judicial process include Kevin T. McGuire, ed., *New Directions in Judicial Politics* (New York: Routledge, 2012); Jeb Barnes, ed., *Judicial Policymaking: Readings on Law, Politics, and Public Policy*, 2nd ed. (San Diego, CA: Cognella Academic, 2016); and Mark C. Miller, *Exploring Judicial Politics* (New York: Oxford University Press, 2008).

Building on these technical works are books that explore various aspects of the American judicial system. Some examples include the following:

On juries: Jeffrey Abramson, *We, the Jury: The Jury System and the Ideal of Democracy* (Cambridge, MA: Harvard University Press, 2000); Andrew Guthrie Ferguson, *Why Jury Duty Matters: A Citizen's Guide to Constitutional Action* (New York: New York University Press, 2012); Neil Vidmar and Valerie P. Hans, *American Juries: The Verdict* (New York: Prometheus, 2007); Reid Hastie et al., *Inside the Jury* (Clark, NJ: Lawbook Exchange, 2013); Hiroshi Fukurai and Richard Krooth, *Race in the Jury Box: Affirmative Action in Jury Selection* (Albany: State University of New York Press, 2003); and Sonali Chakravarti, *Radical Enfranchisement in the Jury Room and Public Life* (Chicago: University Press of Chicago, 2020).

On judicial selection: Greg Goelzhauser, *Judicial Merit Selection: Institutional Design and Performance for State Courts* (Philadelphia: Temple University Press, 2019); Greg Goelzhauser, *Choosing State Supreme Court Justices: Merit Selection and the Consequences of Institutional Reform* (Philadelphia: Temple University Press, 2016); Herbert M. Kritzer, *Justices on the Ballot: Continuity and Change in State Supreme Court Elections* (New York: Cambridge University Press, 2019); Henry J. Abraham,

Justices, Presidents, and Senators: A History of the U.S. Supreme Court Appointments from Washington to Bush II, 5th ed. (Lanham, MD: Rowman & Littlefield, 2007); Renee Knake Jefferson and Hannah Brenner Johnson, *Shortlisted: Women in the Shadows of the Supreme Court* (New York: New York University Press, 2020); Lawrence Baum et al., *The Battle for the Court: Interest Groups, Judicial Elections and Public Policy* (Charlottesville: University Press of Virginia, 2017); and Jed Handelsman Shugerman, *The People's Courts: Pursuing Judicial Independence in America* (Cambridge, MA: Harvard University Press, 2012).

On judicial and legal reasoning: Benjamin Cardozo, *The Nature of the Judicial Process* (New Orleans, LA: Quid Pro, 2010); Richard A. Posner, *How Judges Think*, repr. ed. (Cambridge, MA: Harvard University Press, 2010); and Frederick Schauer, *Thinking Like a Lawyer: A New Introduction to Legal Reasoning*, repr. ed. (Cambridge, MA: Harvard University Press, 2012).

On the US Supreme Court: Linda Greenhouse, *The U.S. Supreme Court: A Very Short Introduction*, 2nd ed. (New York: Oxford University Press, 2020); Keith E. Whittington, *Political Foundations of Judicial Supremacy: The Presidency, the Supreme Court, and Constitutional Leadership in U.S. History* (Princeton, NJ: Princeton University Press, 2009); Peter Charles Hoffer, Willliamjames Hull Hoffer, and N. E. H. Hull, *The Supreme Court: An Essential History*, 2nd ed. (Lawrence: University Press of Kansas, 2018); William H. Rehnquist, *The Supreme Court*, new ed. (New York: Alfred A. Knopf, 2001); and David O'Brien, *Storm Center: The Supreme Court in American Politics*, 12th ed. (New York: W. W. Norton, 2020).

On courts as limited institutions: Gerald N. Rosenberg, *The Hollow Hope: Can Courts Bring About Social Change?*, 2nd ed. (Chicago: University of Chicago Press, 2008); Michael J. Klarman, *From Jim Crow to Civil Rights: The Supreme Court and the Struggle for Racial Equality* (New York: Oxford University Press, 2004); and Donald L. Horowitz, *The Courts and Social Policy* (Washington, DC: Brookings Institution, 1977).

The Internet offers useful sources of information about the structure, powers, and motivations of the judicial system. Some very useful websites include the following: federal courts, Federal Judicial Center, https://www.fjc.gov/history/; state courts, https://www.courts.state.co.us; National Center for State Courts, https://www.ncsc.org/Information-and-Resources/Browse-by-State/

State-Court-Websites.aspx; Court Statistics Project, http://
www.courtstatistics.org; and Bureau of Justice Statistics, https://
www.bjs.gov/index.cfm?ty=tp&tid=30.

Last, there are videos, many online from PBS (or for rent from various
streaming services), on the workings of the judicial system. They
include *Inside the Jury Room* (1986), *This Honorable Court: Part II:
Inside the Marble Temple* (1998), *The Child Terror* (1998), *Snitch*
(1999), *Real Justice* (2000), *Juvenile Justice* (2001), *An Ordinary
Crime* (2002), *The Plea* (2004), *The O. J. Verdict* (2004), *The
Confessions* (2010), and *Supreme Revenge: Battle for the
Court* (2019).

Index

A

Ableman v. Booth, 92
Adkins v. Children's Hospital, 99
administrative agencies, 1, 29
Administrative Procedures Act of
    1946, 52–53
affirmative action, 26
Alabama, 90–91
American Bar Association, 51, 60
appeal by right, 9
appellate court remedies
    affirm, 25, 81
    remand, 25, 81
    reverse, 25, 81
arbitration, 7
Arkansas, 2–3
Article I Courts (Legislative
    Courts), 11, 31, 52–53
Article III Courts (Constitutional
    Courts), 11, 31, 51

B

*Barron v. Mayor & City Council of
    Baltimore*, 100
beyond a reasonable doubt
    standard, 21, 82
Bill of Rights, 64–65, 83, 100
Brooks, Preston, 93

*Brown v. Board of Education of
    Topeka*, 25–26

C

California, 92–93
caseloads, 5, 7, 9–10, 27–28, 37
cases (civil and criminal), 6–7, 12–13
cases of first impression, 40–41
*Charles River Bridge v. Warren
    Bridge*, 92
checks and balances, 86–87, 105–106
Chisholm v. Georgia, 90
Civil Rights Cases, 100–101
Civil War, 96
Cohens v. Virginia, 92
The Common Law, 48
common law of England, 29
complaint, 70–71
Compromise of 1850, 92–93
Congress, 11, 14, 86, 90
courts
    appellate, 2–3, 8, 16, 37
    as sources of change, 34–35
    bankruptcy, 5
    circuit, 2–3, 6
    city and municipal, 18–19
    criminal, 5, 18–19
    district, 2–3, 5–6
    drug, 18–19

family, 17, 19
federal, 5, 13–14, 86
housing, 19
intermediate appellate, 3, 9–10,
    24, 31, 37, 40, 81, 89–90, 106
juvenile, 11, 18–19
magistrate, 5
of common pleas, 6
of equity, 6
of last resort (Supreme Courts),
    2–3, 8–10, 16, 20–21, 27–28,
    31, 37–38, 57, 89, 106
of law, 6
probate, 11, 17, 19–20
small claims, 3–4, 11, 19
specialized, 3, 10
state, 5, 9–12
superior, 6
traffic, 3–4, 11, 17
trial, 2–4, 16
trial courts of general jurisdiction,
    3, 6, 20, 36, 40, 70–71
trial courts of limited or specific
    jurisdiction, 3–5, 7, 11–12,
    17–19, 40
Colorado, 7
contingency fees, 69
Coppage v. Kansas, 99

D

damages, 6, 21–23
Dartmouth College v. Woodward, 92
defendant, 12–14, 21–23, 35, 67
Delaware, 6
discovery, 74, 82
DNA fingerprinting, 40–41
Dred Scott v. Sandord, 94–95

E

Eleventh Amendment, 90
Equal Employment Opportunity
    Commission, 30–31
executive branch agencies, 11

F

Federal Communications
    Commission, 30–31
federal courts, 13–14
    Circuit, 2–3, 11
    District, 2–3, 5–6, 11
    See also, *United States
        Supreme Court*
Federal Tort Claims Act of
    1948, 46
federalism, 14–15
Federalist, no. 78, 33–34
felony, 5
Fifth Amendment, 95
Fifteenth Amendment, 100–101
Fletcher, Robert, 91
forum shopping, 70–71
Fourteenth Amendment, 97–100

G

Galanter, Marc, 36
Georgia, 90–91
Gibbons v. Ogden, 92
Giles v. Harris, 100–101
Grutter v. Bollinger, 26
guilty pleas, 4–5

H

habeas corpus, 42
Hamilton, Alexander, 33–34
Hammer v Dagenhart, 99
Holden v. Hardy, 98
Holmes, Oliver Wendell, Jr.,
    48, 98–99
homicide, 21
Hopwood v. Texas, 26

I

Illinois, 53
Immunity
    charitable, 44

sovereign, 45
testimonial, 44–45
through contract, 46–47
injunction, 21–23
Interstate Commerce Commission,
    30, 96–97

J

Jay, John, 41–42
Judge(s), 4–7, 9, 16, 23–25, 33–34,
    38, 40, 49–50, 76
    attributes, 54
    backgrounds, 50, 56
    judicial philosophies, 50,
        52, 56–57
    nominations and
        confirmation, 51
    selection, 50
    women and minorities, 56
judgments
    default, 7, 72
    on the pleadings, 7
    summary, 7, 73
judicial function(s), 17–29
    administrative, 16, 19–23
    authoritative notice, 2
    dispute resolution, 1–2, 19–23
    enforcement, 2–4, 16, 18–23
    error correction, 9–10, 25–26, 28
    official validation, 2
    policymaking, 10, 16, 28, 37–38
    procedural, 20
    rule definition and
        revision, 10, 37
    sanctioning, 20
    standard setting, 17
judicial panel(s), 9
judicial decision making
    abstention, 43–44
    advisory opinions, 41–42
    case or controversy, 41–42
    conflict of laws, 43–44, 70–71
    immunity, 44
    mootness, 42

political question doctrine, 33
precedent, 23–24, 40
res judicata (claim preclusion), 43
standing, 42
stare decisis, 23–24
statute of limitations, 33
judicial philosophies/ideologies, 57
Judicial Pyramid, 3, 6, 10–11, 17,
    23–24, 35, 37, 49–50, 56
judicial remedies
    common law (damages), 71, 79
    equitable, 71–72, 79
judicial review, 38–40, 89–99
judicial selection
    by appointment, 51
    by election, 53
    by merit, 53
    federal, 51
    state, 53
jurisdiction 3, 11–14, 35–38
    criminal, 14
    diversity, 13–14, 33
    Erie doctrine, 13–14
    federal question, 13–14
    original, 13–14
    removal, 14
    subject matter, 5, 11–14,
        41–42, 70–71
    personal, 11–14, 41–42, 70–71
jury, 49–50, 61–64, 67, 76
    grand, 21, 29, 44–45
    trial or *petit*, 3–4, 6, 20–21,
        61, 79

K

Kansas, 92–93
Kansas-Nebraska Act, 92–93

L

Lawrence v. Texas, 104
lawyer, 49–50, 58–60
    litigator, 59, 68
    transactional, 59

liberty of contract, 98–99
litigants, 6, 33, 35, 49, 67
Lochner, Joseph, 98
Lochner v. New York, 96
Louisiana, 2–3, 26
Louisiana Purchase, 92–93

M

Marbury v. Madison, 27–28, 86
Marshall, John, 27–28, 91
Maryland, 40–41, 94–95
Maryland Court of Appeals,
    40–41
McCulloch v. Maryland, 92
mediation, 7, 75–76
Mexican–American War,
    92–93
Mills v. Green, 100–101
misdemeanors, 5
Mississippi, 6, 26, 90–91
Missouri, 92–93, 95
Missouri Compromise, 92–93, 95
Motions
    answer, 72–73
    complaint, 72
    directed verdict, 79
    dismiss, 72–73, 78
    judgment notwithstanding the
        verdict, 80–81
    new trial, 80–81

N

National Labor Relations
    Board, 30–31
New Jersey, 6
New York, 97
New York Bakeshop Act
    (1895), 97
New York Court of
    Appeals, 2–3
New York Supreme Court, 2–3
Nixon, Richard, 103

O

Obergefell v. Hodges, 104
O'Connor, Sandra Day, 28
"one shotters," 36

P

partisan gerrymanders, 104
Peck, John, 91
personal injury, 68–69
plaintiffs, 12–14, 21–23
plea bargaining, 59–60, 64,
    83–84
Plessy v. Ferguson, 100–101
preponderance of the evidence
    standard, 21–23, 82
President of the United States, 86
Progressive Movement, 97
prosecutor, 21

R

*Regents of the University of
    California v. Bakke*, 26
"repeat players," 36, 58, 68
Reproductive rights, 101–102
rights of the accused, 101
right to privacy, 102
Roberts, John, Jr., 56–57, 104–105
Rucho v. Common Cause, 104–105

S

Scott, Dred, 93
Separation of powers,
    86–87, 105–106
settlement agreements, 7, 9, 64, 70
Sherman Anti-Trust Act, 96–97
Slaughterhouse Cases, 100–101
summons, 72
Sumner, Charles, 93
supremacy clause, 15
Swift v. Tyson, 92

T

Taney, Roger B., 94
Tennessee, 6
testimony, 77
Texas, 2–3, 7, 26
Texas Court of Criminal
    Appeals, 2–3
Texas Railroad Commission, 30
Texas Supreme Court, 2–3
tort, 68
trial
    bench 4–5, 20–21, 76
    jury, 20–21, 76
    civil, 21–23, 67–82
    criminal, 20–21, 23

U

United States Circuit Courts of
    Appeals, 9–10
United States Circuit Court of
    Appeals for the Fifth
    Circuit, 26

United States Circuit Court of
    Appeals for the Ninth Circuit, 27
United States Constitution, 13–14,
    41–42, 85–86
United States Supreme Court, 2–3,
    9–10, 13–14, 26, 28, 40–41,
    43–44, 52, 89–106
United States v. Collazo, 27
Utah, 98

V

voir dire, 61
Voting Rights Act of 1965, 104

W

Washington, George, 41–42
Washington, D. C., 92–93

Y

Yazoo lands, 90–91

THE U.S CONGRESS
A Very Short Introduction
Donald Richie

The world's most powerful national legislature, the U. S. Congress, remains hazy as an institution. This *Very Short Introduction* to Congress highlights the rules, precedents, and practices of the Senate and House of Representatives, and offers glimpses into their committees and floor proceedings to reveal the complex processes by which they enact legislation. In *The U.S. Congress*, Donald A. Ritchie, a congressional historian for more than thirty years, takes readers on a fascinating, behind-the-scenes tour of Capitol Hill-pointing out the key players, explaining their behaviour, and translating parliamentary language into plain English.

www.oup.com/vsi

THE AMERICAN PRESIDENCY
A Very Short Introduction
Charles O. Jones

This marvellously concise survey is packed with information about the presidency, some of it quite surprising. We learn, for example, that the Founders adopted the word "president" over "governor" and other alternatives because it suggested a light hand, as in one who presides, rather than rules. Indeed, the Constitutional Convention first agreed to a weak chief executive elected by congress for one seven-year term, later calling for independent election and separation of powers. Jones sheds much light on how assertive leaders, such as Andrew Jackson, Theodore Roosevelt, and FDR enhanced the power of the presidency, and illuminating how such factors as philosophy (Reagan's anti-Communist conservatism), the legacy of previous presidencies (Jimmy Carter following Watergate), relations with Congress, and the impact of outside events have all influenced presidential authority.

> "In this brief but timely book, a leading expert takes us back to the creation of the presidency and insightfully explains the challenges of executive leadership in a separated powers system."
>
> George C. Edwards III, Distinguished Professor of Political Science, Texas A&M University

www.oup.com/vsi

THE REAGAN REVOLUTION
The Very Short Introduction
Gil Troy

This compact volume identifies and tackles some of the controversies and historical mysteries that continue to swirl around Reagan and his legacy, while providing an illuminating look at some of the era's defining personalities, ideas, and accomplishments. Gil Troy, a well-known historian who is a frequent commentator on contemporary politics, sheds much light on the phenomenon known as the Reagan Revolution, situating the reception of Reagan's actions within the contemporary liberal and conservative political scene. This marvellous book places the Reagan Revolution in the broader context of post-war politics, highlighting the legacies of these years on subsequent presidents and on American life today.

www.oup.com/vsi

AMERICAN POLITICAL PARTIES AND ELECTIONS
A Very Short Introduction
Sandy L. Maisel

Few Americans and even fewer citizens of other nations understand the electoral process in the United States. Still fewer understand the role played by political parties in the electoral process or the ironies within the system. Participation in elections in the United States is much lower than in the vast majority of mature democracies. Perhaps this is because of the lack of competition in a country where only two parties have a true chance of winning, despite the fact that a large number of citizens claim allegiance to neither and think badly of both. Studying these factors, you begin to get a very clear picture indeed of the problems that underlay this much trumpeted electoral system.

www.oup.com/vsi

Religion in America
A Very Short Introduction
Timothy Beal

Timothy Beal describes many aspects of religion in contemporary America that are typically ignored in other books on the subject, including religion in popular culture and counter-cultural groups; the growing phenomenon of "hybrid" religious identities, both individual and collective; the expanding numbers of new religious movements, or NRMs, in America; and interesting examples of "outsider religion." He also offers an engaging overview of the history of religion in America, from Native American traditions to the present day. Finally, Beal highlights the three major forces shaping the present and future of religion in America.

www.oup.com/vsi